A Glimpse *of* Light

THE BASICS OF THE
WISDOM OF KABBALAH

A Glimpse *of* Light

THE BASICS OF THE
WISDOM OF KABBALAH

Laitman
Kabbalah
Publishers

Michael Laitman, PhD

A Glimpse of Light: the basics of the wisdom of kabbalah
Copyright © 2013 by Michael Laitman

Published by Laitman Kabbalah Publishers
www.kabbalah.info   info@kabbalah.info
1057 Steeles Avenue West, Suite 532, Toronto, ON,
M2R 3X1, Canada
2009 85th Street #51, Brooklyn, New York, 11214, USA

Printed in Canada

ISBN - 978-1-897448-83-0
Library of Congress Control Number: 2013904822

Translation: Susan Gal
Associate Editor: Chaim Ratz
Proofreading: Mary Miesem
Copy Editor: Claire Gerus
Layout: Baruch Khovov
Cover: Studio Yaniv, Inna Smirnova
Executive Editor: Oren Levi
Printing and Post Production: Uri Laitman

FIRST EDITION: JANUARY 2014
First printing

CONTENTS

About the Book

A *Glimpse of Light* is a compilation of selected contemplations from the ocean of wisdom offered in the wisdom of Kabbalah. This book touches upon topics such as pleasure, ego, love, men and women, globalization, education, ecology, Nature, perception of reality, *The Book of Zohar*, and spirituality. A *Glimpse of Light* presents the unique approach of Kabbalah to familiar concepts such as The Creator, *Adam HaRishon*, the Nation of Israel, the Torah, the righteous, and prayer.

The book came about from our wish to share the sublime experience of studying Kabbalah with our readers. Every day, we collected the items that touched our hearts the most in Dr. Michael Laitman's Kabbalah lessons. His teachings on *The Book of Zohar*, the writings of The Ari, and the writings of Rav Yehuda Ashlag (Baal HaSulam) are broadcast live on a daily basis to thousands of viewers throughout the world on www. kab.tv and www.kabbalah.info.

We compiled the material by topics. Just open the book wherever you wish, and begin to read. Each chapter contains several sections that combine to form a complete picture. At times, frequent Q&A are given to help clarify the issues under discussion. We present this collection to you as a "glimpse of the Light," so you may sense the profound emotions and perceptions that we can all attain by studying the wisdom of Kabbalah.

The Editors

Foreword

We are witnessing the turmoil the world is going through in all areas of life: natural disasters, global crises, and acute social crises in education and human relations. Materialistically speaking, we have the benefit of abundance unavailable to previous generations, yet there is an odd sense of tastelessness in the air.

Some people feel this is just another transient, turbulent period, but according to the wisdom of Kabbalah, that is not the case. We are living in a historic time, a moment before we burst forth into a new life. It is a difficult time, filled with labor pains, and Kabbalah is being revealed in order to assist us, just as an experienced midwife would do.

The wisdom of Kabbalah developed in ancient Babel. At that time, humanity lived as one big clan. Then, unexpectedly, the ego burst forth, as described in the story of the Tower of Babel.

In Babel, a wise man named Abraham began to study the events of his time and developed the wisdom of Kabbalah. Abraham's wisdom is a science that familiarizes us with the secret "control room" of the universe, teaches us what is happening to us, and tells us how to control our lives.

With the world now a global village, as it was in ancient Babel, it is again difficult for us to get along with each other. It is as if we are crammed together in a pressure cooker, not knowing how to get out of it. The Kabbalists foresaw this situation and pointed to these times as "the turning point at which the wisdom of Kabbalah would be revealed to the masses," to offer an explanation and a solution to our problems.

Throughout the millennia during which Kabbalah was concealed, many false notions became associated with it. As a result, people thought it was a mystical system dealing with spells and witchcraft, amulets and supernatural cures, red strings, holy water and so on. In truth, it is a scientific method that reveals the system behind the forces of Nature governing our world.

The wisdom of Kabbalah explains everything that has happened, is happening, and will happen to us— from the global level, through the family unit, and down to the inner point situated deep in each of our hearts, which feels we deserve the best that life can offer.

Rabbi Menachem Mendel of Kotzk

"Man was made to lift up the Heavens."

The wisdom of Kabbalah has been revealed in our generation by virtue of the great Kabbalist of the twentieth century, Rav Yehuda Ashlag (1884-1954). Rav Ashlag, known as Baal HaSulam (Owner of the Ladder) for his *Sulam* (Ladder) commentary on *The Book of Zohar*, wrote in his twilight years, the *Writings of the Last Generation*. In the introduction to his revolutionary composition, he wrote: "There is an allegory about friends who were lost in the desert, hungry and thirsty. One of them had found a settlement filled abundantly with every delight. ...So is the matter before us: we have been lost in the terrible desert along with all of humanity, and now we have found a great, abundant treasure, namely the books of Kabbalah in the treasure. ...Now, distinguished readers, this book lies here before you in a closet. It states explicitly all the wisdom of statesmanship and the behavior of private and public life that will exist at the end of days."

Kabbalah and Us

TURNING TOWARD NATURE

There is a positive force in Nature. The wisdom of Kabbalah teaches us how to be wise and receive that force so it develops us correctly and well.

Kabbalah does not speak of any artificial situations or abstract notions. It explains how we should build ourselves, and what type of interconnected network we should create so we can receive the inclusive force that exists in Nature with greater intensity. At present, we seem to be turning our backs on that force, and we have to learn how to turn around and face it.

THE LAW OF ROOTS AND BRANCHES

"Thus, there is not an element of reality, or an occurrence of reality in a lower world, that you

*will not find its likeness in the world above it, as
identical as two drops in a pond. And they are
called 'Root and Branch.'"*

Baal HaSulam, "The Essence of the Wisdom of Kabbalah"

The "Law of Roots and Branches" is one of the fundamental
laws in the wisdom of Kabbalah. It states that every action,
thought, desire, or occurrence, everything in our world,
from particles in atoms through human beings and up
to entire galaxies, is operated by forces from above. The
relation between the forces and the things they affect is
one of cause and effect, root and branch.

The wisdom of Kabbalah allows us to reveal the Upper
World, in which the roots of everything occurring in
our world exist. When we reveal those roots, the world
seems to become transparent. We see the forces that
activate everything. We begin to feel where our thoughts
and desires come from, why certain things happen to us
or to others. We see how the network of forces operates
in the world, and how it governs every occurrence here
with the "waves" emanating from it.

At every moment, even now, we are living in an image
that those forces build for us. They activate us from
within and from without just like marionettes, without
us being aware of it. Now we have the opportunity to
locate the place within that image through which we can

enter and begin to influence those forces reciprocally, thus learning to govern life.

WHY WAS THE WISDOM HIDDEN?

"I am glad that I have been born in such a generation when it is permitted to disclose the wisdom of truth."

Baal HaSulam, "The Teaching of the Kabbalah and Its Essence"

The wisdom of Kabbalah was hidden from the public until today because it was necessary to wait until we developed to a state where our lives didn't look so great anymore. A few decades ago, people still felt thankful to science and culture; they were making achievements, thriving, and developing. Life seemed promising, and it appeared that our children would have it even better.

Today, it seems as if we have reached a dead end. We are surrounded by dangers, and the ecological situation seems ominous, as well. The hope of a better life is dissipating. Our growing hopelessness makes us ready to accept the explanation that Kabbalah offers us as to the origin of our problems and their solution.

Kabbalah explains that after thousands of years of egoistic development, the world has reached a state in which, on the one hand, everyone is connected to each other, and on the other hand, are hateful toward each other. We are incarcerated in a cage with nowhere to run. Clearly, we are suffering because of it, but it isn't clear to us how we can stop the decline.

This situation is no coincidence; it is a predetermined step in the development plan of Creation. It is meant to promote us to the next degree of our existence.

A NEW GENERATION, A NEW DIMENSION

The whole of the wisdom of Kabbalah is only to know the guidance of the Higher Will, why It has created all these creatures, what It wants with them, and what the end of all the cycles of the world will be.

Ramchal, *138 Doors of Wisdom*, Section 30

We are living at a very special time. After thousands of years of concealment, the authentic wisdom of Kabbalah is again being revealed to all, to any person, whoever he or she may be, without any preconditions.

People are beginning to understand that the purpose of the method of Kabbalah is to elevate us to the highest degree in Nature, the degree of the Creator. In other words, Kabbalah is not for teaching magic or tricks, remedies, amulets, cures or blessings, nor is it to improve our corporeal life. Rather, it is meant to elevate us to a new level of existence.

With Kabbalah, we come to know the supreme plan of Creation, we understand what is the goal of our existence on the earth, and what we must do to realize our potential. All of humanity should attain that unique and superior state in our time.

Ego

CROSSING EVERY LINE

Today, we have reached a state in which the ego controls people and doesn't let them be considerate of others. Even the rule, "That which you hate, do not do to your friend," has been drained of content. Until now, that rule has served us in our daily lives. For instance, we avoided harming our neighbors so they wouldn't harm us. The ego warned us: "Leave the neighbor alone or you will suffer vengeance." This is how the neighbor felt, as well, so life was running in an orderly manner.

We lived that way for generations. Although at times we felt a little constrained, people tended to agree that it was the best way to live. But these days, the ego has overflowed, breaking all the boundaries among us, beyond every fence and wall of defense. It is simply bursting, and as a result, we are already incapable of controlling ourselves.

People will do anything to succeed. The overuse of the ego has become a social norm, and the media exalts those phenomena. Everything is permissible, as long as it succeeds.

We need to understand this process in greater depth. There are no good people or bad people; there is a development intended to force us to realize the destructiveness of egoism and the urgent need to correct it.

A DIFFERENT TYPE OF GIVING

Man's very essence is only to receive for oneself.
By nature, we are unable to do even the smallest
thing to benefit others. Instead, when we give to
others, we are compelled to expect that in the end,
we will receive a worthwhile reward.

Baal HaSulam,
"A Speech for the Completion of The Zohar"

We all think of ourselves first. Even when we help others, give something, or treat others nicely, it is in order to receive something in return.

If we do something good for others, it is because it somehow pays off. We think along the lines of, "They will also help me when I am old or sick," or "If I help someone else's child across the street, they will also help mine," or "That way, the world will be better and more comfortable for me and my family."

Today, however, Nature's plan of development is demanding that we rise above narrow, individual payoffs to reach the highest degree of reality, the degree of love and pure giving.

WHAT TRUE EGO ACTUALLY IS

When I want to eat, drink, be with my family, have a good job, vacation, these are not considered egoism. The desire to enjoy corporeal pleasures, things we need in order to have a comfortable, safe, healthy life, are not what the term "ego" means, according to the wisdom of Kabbalah.

According to Kabbalah, egoism is when a person wants to harm another person. Ego is the hatred of others, the opposite of the inclusive law of reality, "Love your friend as yourself."

TEST YOURSELF

The still, vegetative, and animate constantly search to secure their existence, seeking food, a habitat, and so on. And yet, they are not considered egoists. Why not? Because they receive from the world only what Nature requires them to receive, and not beyond.

The ego exists only in the human race, in which the desire to use others is revealed. When I don't find being happy is sufficient, and I want others to be unhappy; when I want to feel superior and to use others for my own satisfaction, this is called "egoism."

However, nothing can be said to a person on this matter; in this work, one must judge and analyze oneself. The wisdom of Kabbalah helps us study and know ourselves. No one will tell you, "You're an egoist." Rather, you, yourself will begin to observe where your thoughts are directed.

WOLVES, DEER AND SATISFACTION IN LIFE

Does a wolf that preys on a deer hate it? No. Does the deer hate the wolf? No. The wolf sees the deer as food it needs to eat. Obviously, the deer resists, but it can't be said that there is hatred between them.

To human eyes, the wolf gets little pleasure from eating the deer while filling its belly. But when we humans overcome an enemy, our joy is much greater and deeper because the human struggle is accompanied by intense feelings of hatred, competition, power struggles, and pursuit of honor. In other words, unlike the wolf, which wants only the deer's flesh, we aren't satisfied until we also "take" our enemy's "heart."

> *"The equal side in all the people of the world is that each of us stands ready to abuse and exploit all the people for our own private benefit with every means possible, without taking into any consideration that we are going to build ourselves on the ruin of friends, and it makes no difference what permission we conjures up for ourselves."*
>
> Baal HaSulam, "Peace in the World"

DON'T DESTROY THE EGO!

When we delve into the perceptions of religions and teachings developed through the ages, we discover that they are based on diminishing the ego. A person should "calm" himself as much as possible, be pleasant to others, accept everything submissively, and so on.

The wisdom of Kabbalah says the exact opposite. We mustn't destroy the ego. Throughout history we've been developing it, so why should we suddenly destroy it? I want to use the entire world, defeat everyone, be the smartest, most successful person on the planet, stuff myself with every kind of satisfaction. This is precisely what was meant by the maxim, "He who is greater than his friend, his inclination is greater than him."[1]

If we destroy the ego, we'll have nothing to correct because we won't be ourselves anymore, as if we disappeared. Every spiritual ascent is achieved only over hatred. This is what the term "Mount Sinai" symbolizes—the mountain of *Sinaa* (hatred) within us. The more we discover the hatred and the ego hidden within, and learn to use them properly, the higher we will ascend. But that ascent depends on our seeing our ego as a force coming to our assistance, or "help made against him."

In short, our true work is to use everything that has been created, the full power of the ego. It is with good reason that man was created the most egoistic creature in Nature, and it is with good reason that we received the wisdom of Kabbalah, the method of correction, so we may use it to correct our egos.

> *"Everything in reality, good and bad, and even the most harmful in the world, has a right to exist and should not be eradicated from the world. We must only mend and reform it."*
>
> **Baal HaSulam, "Peace in the World"**

GROW, GROW, AND GROW

Question: It seems like Kabbalah speaks a great deal about the ego. Why is that?

Kabbalah speaks a great deal about the ego because it is the fundamental matter of Creation. The ego is connected to the person's self, and includes the heart and the intellect. The heart symbolizes our desires, and the intellect symbolizes our thoughts. This is why whoever wants to develop should direct the heart and the intellect toward unity with others.

When I unite with others in the way that the wisdom of Kabbalah teaches, I begin to feel their desires and thoughts. This is how I grow. I begin to include all the desires and thoughts in the world within me. Imagine how much each of us could expand inside, and the more we grow within, the more pleasure we sense.

Adam HaRishon

LIGHT OUT OF THE DARKNESS

Nature's all-inclusive force is one of love and giving. In Kabbalah, it is called the "Creator" or the "Upper Light." Initially, the Creator created one reality called *Adam HaRishon* (The First Man). One *Adam* (man) means one desire, not one human being, but one spiritual system.

As our body consists of billions of parts, that one desire includes billions of desires, all of which connect into a vast system.

Initially, the parts of this system operated in harmony and were as one, but that harmony was actually caused by the Upper Light. Next, an act called "shattering" occurred and the Light disappeared from the single desire it had created. The desire that remained without the imparting of the Light is considered shattered. More precisely, in itself each piece still seemed whole, but the connection between the pieces was shattered. It was a meltdown, where pieces stopped working with one another. It became impossible to receive or to give, and the system became dysfunctional.

What did we gain from the shattering? We gained our ego. That is, on the one hand, the more we hate each other and grow distant from each other, the more we are devoid of Light. On the other hand, only out of that state of darkness can we understand what is the Light, and what is the Creator. It was said about that understanding through opposites, "As the advantage of the Light out of the darkness."[2] Indeed, only out of the difference, the contrast between those two states can we begin to understand and attain the Creator.

A COMPLETE HUMAN BEING

"The Upper Will wished for man to complement himself and all that was created for him, and that itself would be his merit and reward...For in the end, he will be the whole one, and will delight in the pleasure for all of eternity."

Ramchal,
Daat Tevunot [Knowledge of Intelligence], 14

Why did the Creator shatter the single creature He created, the collective soul? Actually, sometimes we do it to our children when we want to help them develop. For example, to create a puzzle we first draw a picture, and then cut it into pieces. The children try to put the pieces together by themselves, and develop in the process. Similarly, only when we reunite into a single, complete human being will we be able to understand Creation.

It is important to understand that there is a huge qualitative difference between the collective soul prior to its shattering and after its correction. We will illustrate that with an example. A TV set is a complicated instrument, but everyone knows how to operate it. Suppose the television broke into little pieces, and for some reason I had no choice but to fix it. Think how smart I'd be after fixing it! I'd have to know its structure, the plastic and metal pieces, the wires, the connections, and how they all connected. After all, we are talking about total shattering, so I'd have to know everything in order to fix it.

Once I understand how it is built, I begin to be aware of the one who planned and manufactured it. Indeed, he invested his "all" into his creation, so by following his actions, I understand and attain him.

Thus, rather than having basic knowledge which button to press and when, I put together the whole of Creation by myself and all of Creation becomes mine. By doing so, I acquire the Creator's intelligence and His stature.

ALL THE GOOD AND THE PLEASURABLE

"The Creator's desired goal for the Creation He had created is to bestow upon His creatures, so they would know His truthfulness and greatness, and receive all the delight and pleasure He had prepared for them."

Baal HaSulam, "Introduction to the Book of Zohar," [39]

The single soul divided into numerous souls in order to give each and every one of us the chance to resemble the Creator. The Creator has the desire to give, and we are made of the desire to receive. This is our nature.

What is bad about being the receiver? When I receive, my desire is neutralized by the pleasure of reception. We see it in our own lives. Suppose I want a fancy car and I work for years to save enough to buy it. When I finally do, I sit in it, enjoying myself after having worked for it for so long. I cherish every knob in the car and admire it with my eyes.

But a few weeks after the purchase, the pleasure dissipates. I've become accustomed to the car and it seems to have lost its charm.

We're all familiar with that process. It is how the will to receive is built. We chase pleasures, each time a different one, until we tire of the race, and then we die. Yes, yes, that is truly how it is. People die when they are tired of life.

Feeling eternal pleasure means having an eternal life. Is it possible to live forever? Can a person achieve a degree of being like the Creator, eternal and complete? For that, one must come to a state of receiving boundless filling, which must constantly increase. Moreover, it mustn't increase out of a feeling of lack—it must grow from good to better, then to better still. We can't even fathom the possibility of not having a sense of lack when between one good thing and another. It is something that we cannot experience in our regular lives.

How can it be done? For that, the Creator took the huge vessel He had created, the will to receive, and divided it into myriad tiny parts, each of which was seemingly closed in itself, disconnected from the other parts. That process was "the breaking of the vessels." As a result, each part regarded itself as the only one that was important, with the other parts existing only to benefit it.

Why was that done? It was done because now I am able to change my attitude toward others all by myself. I can change my approach to others and turn it into one similar to a mother's approach toward her children. I need to come to a state where I feel all the other desires as though they were mine.

When I achieve that, I acquire the entire vessel that the Creator created. Everyone is like my own children; I love them and I satiate them. Infinite lights traverse me, filling the great vessel that I feel as my own, as me. Thus, I have attained an endless, boundless flow, and in that I am similar to the Creator. I have achieved His stature, I became like Him—good and benevolent.

ANTERIOR AND POSTERIOR

Let's imagine that all the people in the world are connected and that we are close to each other, like kin. How would we treat each other? Everything would suddenly fall into place.

Beforehand, I hated you and you hated me, so I had to keep my distance. But now I've discovered that we are truly connected; we are one body. In such a state, harming others means harming me. It might be difficult to imagine, but it's the revelation that the wisdom of Kabbalah brings to people, the revelation of the system of *Adam HaRishon*.

There are two states to the revelation of that system in our world, anterior and posterior. These days the system has already begun to appear, though for now only its posterior side. As a result, the connections among countries and people are being revealed. We are living in a small, global village where everyone affects everyone. The problem is that currently, rejection, hatred, fear, distance, strife, and struggle exist among us, revealing the posterior side of the connection.

If we revealed the system of *Adam HaRishon* on its anterior side, all evil would immediately cease and we would all feel as one. In that state, you can't do anything except what you would do for yourself. You don't feel that others exist; everything becomes a single body; everything is you. This is the revelation that the world needs, and this is why the wisdom of Kabbalah is being revealed today.

THE LIGHT THAT REFORMS

The corrected system we are supposed to reveal is an integrated system. All its parts are interconnected, interrelated. The law sustaining the system is love, bestowal, mutual guarantee.

We are currently situated in a shattered system, and we have to advance toward the corrected system, which serves us as a role model we would like to emulate. At the end of the process, the shattered system will return to being the corrected system, meaning both systems will unite.

The corrected system is described in the texts of Kabbalah. When we study it and desire to advance toward it, our efforts arouse a special force operating upon us, a force called "the Light that reforms." It is a correcting force projected upon us from the corrected system, and its intensity depends on the extent to which we desire to push ourselves in the right direction.

Love

WHAT IS LOVE?

I love what I enjoy. I enjoy my children, good food, and many other things. I love all of them.

In spirituality, love carries a different meaning. Love is an urge to give, bestow, and fill.

Even in our egoistic world, love manifests as an urge to do good things to whomever we love, but it is based on it being pleasant or worthwhile to me. This means that something is forcing me to act that way.

In spirituality, nothing forces you. It is unconditional love, and it is above our nature.

> *"Any movement that a person makes to love*
> *another is performed with a Reflected Light, and*
> *some reward that will eventually return to him*
> *and serve him for his own good. Thus, such an act*

cannot be considered 'love of another' because it is judged by its end."

Baal HaSulam, *Matan Torah* [The Giving of the Torah]

THE DESIRE TO LOVE

When something attracts me, when it arouses in me a sense of possible pleasure, I approach it. The future fulfillment shines for me from afar, and I want to bond with it. This is how we are attracted to what or to whom we believe will bring us pleasure, and we call it "love."

Kabbalah teaches us that the only matter created, the matter from which all of us are made, is "the will to receive delight and pleasure." Accordingly, self-love is defined as the fulfillment of my desire, and love of others is the aspiration to fulfill the desire of others. In other words, either I act in order to satisfy my own desire for pleasure through others, or I act in order to satisfy the desires of others for pleasure, through me.

LOVE AND BESTOWAL

"All our work is to disclose the love between us each and every day."

Baal HaSulam, Letter no. 2

The wisdom of Kabbalah often uses the words "love" and "bestowal" (in the sense of bringing abundance, inundating goodness). Love is an approach and bestowal is an act.

Let's take two people, each with a desire. If I can connect your desire to mine, and consider your desire more important than mine so that my desire will act as a servant to satisfy yours, it is considered that I love you. When I use that love and actualize it, it is regarded as me carrying out an act of "bestowal."

This is what is required of us because we are all parts of a single, global system, *Adam HaRishon*. In it, we are all connected as one. Because of the shattering, we have become removed from each other; the ego has come between us, causing remoteness. For that distance to be eliminated, we must now arrive at an inner demand of our own.

However, eliminating the distance is not done by canceling the ego. Rather, although the ego exists, I want to leap over it. Moreover, I want to use it to strengthen the connection between us.

When both our egos remain between us and we connect above them, we attain a system in which the connections are far stronger than they were initially, in *Adam HaRishon*. By that, we obtain immense pleasure and become equal to the Creator. This is what we acquire through love and bestowal.

> *"When one is imparted the will to bestow, he is qualified to receive the Upper Abundance."*
>
> Baal HaSulam, *Shamati*, Essay 16

WITHOUT COERCION

Question: Suppose a person realizes that he wants to love others. How can he also love people who are difficult to love? How can evil people be loved?

None of us genuinely loves others. We can make believe that we do, but it won't change the fact that we were created with a nature of self-love. Here the wisdom of Kabbalah explains that we mustn't force ourselves and coercively love someone. All we need is to open the Kabbalah books and study.

By studying, we begin to feel a new world. As if out of a mist, the connection between us is revealed. We suddenly feel and see how we are all connected. We begin to discover that everyone is an inseparable part of everyone else. We can't cut off any part; it is not in our power, and no part is redundant in our body. We begin to feel that it is an eternal network of connections in which we are all connected forever.

A unique connection is revealed to us, naturally obligating us to love, and we can no longer refrain from loving others. Love is much more powerful than any connection we are familiar with today. In our world, a person may disconnect from his family and seemingly wipe them out of one's life. Here, it is impossible. The image of connections that appear stands before us in our hearts and emotions, leading us to the love of others.

In short, the wisdom of Kabbalah doesn't require us to do anything artificial. If we use this method correctly, the true connection between us will be revealed and true love will be born within us.

"Love does not come by coercion or compulsion."

Baal HaSulam,
"Introduction to the Study of the Ten Sephirot," Item 82

A REALITY OF LOVE

With the method of Kabbalah, we gradually build the quality of unconditional love within us. That quality enables us to feel our origin, the harmonious, complete, and eternal life, the *Ein Sof* [infinity] that exists beyond physical life.

Within us, we can only feel the minute and brief reality of a few short years. When we emerge from ourselves through the quality of love, we feel a different reality. It is a boundless, infinite reality. It has nothing to do with our bodies, hence there is no life or death in it. It is eternal and harmonious because everything is connected with everything—the positive and negative phenomena unite as one, and there are no contradictions. Everything complements each other. This is perfection, the sublime harmony of Nature.

"Everything stands on love."

The Book of Zohar,
Parashat Va'etchanan [And I Pleaded], Item 126

Creator

THE ALL-INCLUSIVE FORCE OF NATURE

Question: I was taught that the Creator is in heaven, like a kind grandfather. Is it true?

This has been the approach of humanity for generations. It is an approach that says there is some force, but no one knows what it is, so we attribute to that hidden force a character based on our understanding.

The truth is that the Creator is the all-inclusive Force of Nature, as explained in the wisdom of Kabbalah.[3] But since Kabbalah was concealed for thousands of years, we developed misperceptions, believing that if we ask the Creator nicely, He will reward us.

We want to use the Upper Force for our own benefit. We put our trust in Him, as if He were a person. We think, "I'll give Him something, and He'll reciprocate the favor." We think that this way we can bribe Him and all will be well.

This is the common approach, rooted in us through the centuries of exile, the years of detachment from the attainment of the Creator and the feeling of the Upper World.

Exile is a state of concealment, of detachment from spiritual attainment. But today, the wisdom of Kabbalah is being revealed again, clarifying the correct approach to the term, "Creator."

THE RUNGS OF THE LADDER

"Evil, in general, is nothing more than self-love,
called "egoism," as it is opposite in form from the
Creator, who hasn't any will to receive for Himself,
but only to bestow."

Baal HaSulam, "The Essence of Religion and its Purpose"

The Creator is the general force of love and giving, which created the creature as a force of reception, an egoistic will to receive. Both these forces stand one opposite the other like heaven and earth, and a ladder stands between them.

When a person adapts his qualities to those existing at a higher rung on the ladder, he climbs to that higher rung. And when he adapts himself to the next rung, he climbs accordingly.

Everything is in our hands. We've been given the key to Nature, a method of shifting our egoistic nature according to the nature of the Upper Force.

> *"Pleasure is only the equivalence of form with its Maker. And when we equalize with every conduct in our root, we sense delight."*
>
> Baal HaSulam, *Matan Torah* [The Giving of the Torah]

BEING LIKE THE CREATOR

Question: In Kabbalah, we speak about resembling the Creator. How can a person even think that it is possible to resemble the Creator?

No one asked us whether we would like to resemble the Creator or not. It is simply the goal of Creation as determined by the Creator. By the way, no one asked us whether we'd like to be born either, when, where, to which family, or under what conditions.

And as for being similar to the Creator, it isn't as impossible as it might seem right now. We are talking about the force of love and giving that must develop among us. When we are rewarded with it, within that love between us we will also feel we have built that initial force of Nature.

> *All the conducts of Creation, in its every corner, inlet, and outlet, are completely prearranged for the purpose of nurturing the human species from its midst, to improve its qualities until it can sense the Creator as one feels one's friend. These ascensions are like rungs of a ladder, arranged degree-by-degree until it is completed and achieves its purpose.*
>
> Baal HaSulam,
> "The Teaching of the Kabbalah and Its Essence"

CREATOR–COME AND SEE

The Upper Force is called "Creator" because He created everything and sustains everything, and because the people who discovered Him called Him "Creator," from the Hebrew words *Bo Re'eh* [come and see].

"Come" means that you can draw near to Him through "equivalence of form," by equalizing your qualities to His. You execute various inner actions to draw nearer to Him, to feel Him more and more. "See" means that you will know Him. "Sight," in the wisdom of Kabbalah, is the highest level of attainment.

THE TORAH SPOKE IN THE LANGUAGE OF PEOPLE

In the Holy Scriptures there are expressions such as "bringing contentment to the Creator." Indeed, why does the Creator require people to work for Him? It is quite annoying to work for someone.

The thing is that this particular "someone" is the general force of Nature, which includes me, you, everyone, and anything we could possibly imagine, everything! There is nothing but that force. When one acts with the goal of bringing contentment to the Creator, he or she doesn't do it for someone else, but to reveal to oneself and to others the control of that force over the entire Creation.

The Creator neither needs nor receives anything from anyone.[4] He is the will to bestow, the desire to give (not a desire to receive, like us), which is why He can't receive anything from us. We don't really have to do "Him" any "favors," such as cleaving to Him or loving Him. It is written that we should, but only because "'the Torah spoke in the language of people.'"

In an instruction such as, "And you shall love the Lord your God," it concerns only the correction we should make in our own qualities, in our vessels, in order to attain the love of the Creator, meaning to be in equivalence with Him so we may feel the Upper abundance.

> *"When we correct our vessels of reception to be in order to bestow, we thus equalize our Kelim [vessels] to their Maker and become fit to receive His abundance boundlessly."*
>
> Baal HaSulam, *The Study of the Ten Sephirot*, Part I, "Inner Reflection," item 22

THE END OF AN ACT IS IN THE PRELIMINARY THOUGHT

When we want to build a house, we first turn to an architect. He asks us what we want, and we need to describe to him the house we envision: the number of rooms, the style of the house, and so on. The architect suggests several options, helps us decide, and in the end an image of the future house is created.

The course of action at each and every stage throughout the process of construction derives from that image: which building materials to buy, what to do, when, and how. We don't start construction before we have a plan. "The end of an act is in the preliminary thought."

That is precisely how the development of Creation operates. From the beginning, the final form—the state of our perfection—already exists. There, we all exist in the eternal degree; we are all corrected, beautiful, and good. This is the end of the road.

But then, that end is hidden from us and we start from the beginning. Why? So we may reach that end through our own labor, seeking for ourselves, in order to realize that this is what should be done, and not otherwise.

And when we reach the end we discover that, "Wow! We really do already exist here. It has been like that from the beginning."

THE THOUGHT OF CREATION

"This entire reality, Upper and lower as one, in the final state of the end of correction, was emanated and created by a Single Thought. That Single Thought performs all the operations, is the Essence of all the operations, the ultimate Objective, and the Essence of the labor. It is by itself the very perfection and the sought-after reward."

Baal HaSulam, *The Study of the Ten Sephirot*, Part I, "Inner Reflection," item 8

A person who corrects himself sees the Creator's work in everything, the act of the Light building for Itself a place to be revealed to us. Such a person sees that Light as the Thought of Creation, as a single thought operating in reality. He feels the essence of the existence of everything, understands how that thought operates, changing everything in order to be revealed in every single detail, and in all of them together.

Such a person discovers how the Light operates upon all people internally, how It changes them, cleanses them, making them more sensitive, and develops their ability to understand and observe more of Its acts upon them.

CORRELATING EXPECTATIONS

Question: How can I determine which of my plans suits the Creator's plan and which do not, before I carry them out?

First, you should examine the Creator's plan and take something from it to your own plans. In such a case, there will surely be correlation, not the other way around.

Spiritual Globalization

A SPRINGBOARD

If we want to continue living on this planet, we need to examine ourselves and achieve a true change. We have encountered a global crisis in all areas of life: ecology, security, finance, education, and society. The world crisis befalling us is evident on the personal level, as well. There are problems in every family—in health, provisions, relationships, education, and communication with the children. Emptiness and depression are spreading everywhere, and violence is on the rise. It seems as if everything is falling apart at once.

The wisdom of Kabbalah explains that the state we have reached is no coincidence. It is preordained in the development plan for the human race. We aren't to blame for anything; we had to deteriorate to this all-time low. We are at the end of the "decline of the generations" that the Kabbalists foresaw in their writings. At long last, we have reached the turning point, from which a wondrous ascent awaits us. Only a global crisis could have been our springboard to a new and far better state of abundance and prosperity.

> "These negative forces being revealed are the causes of progress in humanity, by which it climbs and ascends as if on rungs of a ladder. And they are surely destined to do their job, to bring humanity to the final stage of development, which is that aspired state, which is clear of any blemish or fault."

Baal HaSulam, from the paper, *The Nation*

LOSING THE WAY

No one understands what's happening to the world, neither the leaders, nor the wise, nor the powerful ones. No one. There have always been those who thought they knew what to do, how to turn the world into a better place and which revolutions and changes to carry out, but today everyone is clueless.

We are observing what is happening and we are helpless; we have no control. Even systems we built by ourselves, such as the economic system, have gone out of control. We invented money, the banking system, insurance companies, and pension funds; yet, we cannot control what is happening.

Nobody knows what will happen tomorrow, which bubble will burst in our faces and collapse the global economy. It's no longer possible to control human egoism or to stop the corruption, embezzlement, and greed. We are damaging ourselves by ourselves, and there is nothing we can do to stop it.

Our era is very special—the era of revealing the evil. And when the illness is apparent, the remedy appears— the wisdom of Kabbalah.

TWO OPPOSITE NETWORKS

*"When each and every individual understands
that his own benefit and the benefit of the
collective are one and same thing, the world will
come to its full correction."*

Baal HaSulam, "Peace in the World"

The world has become a small global village. As a result, we are required to behave as integrated parts in a system. But we are not.

Kabbalah says that the global crisis is the result of a collision between two opposite systems. It is true that we are connected, but in a reverse manner. Our connections are egoistic and exploitive, rather than ones of mutual concern. This inversion causes processes to which we are accustomed—such as economic ones—to suddenly become dysfunctional. We are trying to manage the new system with the old rules, and this is why it isn't working.

WHAT IS GLOBALIZATION?

We tend to perceive globalization as an expansion of financial connections among countries. One country manufactures cars, another focuses on agriculture, a third is blessed with natural resources, and a fourth excels in hi-tech. They trade with each other and everyone benefits.

According to the wisdom of Kabbalah, globalization is indeed a connection, but not only on the level of transferring merchandise, sharing knowledge, or cultural ties. Globalization is an internal connection, a revelation of the network of connections that ties the hearts of all humans everywhere.

Nowadays, we have reached a new level of ego where that network of connections among us is appearing. It is as if we were bound to each other with iron chains. Until now, we wandered around freely, and suddenly we are tied together. Even if we stop transferring merchandise among us, that network will still exist. It cannot be undone. That network is appearing today from within, suddenly popping up from below the surface and tightly gripping each and every one of us, showing us that we are connected to each other with inner ropes that cannot be untied. We are forever connected.

What do we do? We must learn to get along in this new world. The more we know about the global law governing the single system, the fewer blows we will suffer. We have to learn our lives anew, learn how to treat everything around us properly, and how to treat the global nature.

> *"Each and every individual in society is like*
> *a wheel that is linked to several other wheels,*
> *placed in a machine. And this single wheel has*
> *no freedom of movement in and of itself, but*
> *continues with the motion of the rest of the wheels*
> *in a certain direction, to qualify the machine to*
> *perform its general role."*

Baal HaSulam, "Peace in the World"

NOWHERE TO RUN

In a state of a global, financial crisis, each country thinks how good it would be if it could separate itself from the others and have everything it needs for its sustenance, just as it was a hundred years ago. We'll turn back time, make things the way they were before; we'll place high tariffs on imports, trade with other countries only for minimal necessities, and freeze business connections. We'll live more simply, but at least we will be less dependent on others.

We don't realize that there is no turning back, and countries that separate themselves will endure even bigger blows. They won't understand where these came from, when actually they will have come from the inclusive force of Nature. It's like a part of the body that wants to cut itself from the body in order to be saved from a disease that attacked the body. Could it exist on its own?

> *"We can no longer speak or deal with just conducts that promise the well-being of one country or one nation, but only the well-being of the whole world because the benefit or harm of each and every person in the world depends and is measured by the benefit of all the people in the whole world."*
>
> Baal HaSulam, "Peace in the World"

NUCLEAR ENERGY

The power of nuclear energy has been revealed in order to show us how connected all of us are to each other. Anything that happens at one end of the earth affects everyone, whether we want it to or not, as the disaster in Japan clearly indicated. In the era of nuclear energy, which already provides 9% of the global energy needs, it is very clear that we are all sitting in one boat.

WE NEED HELP

We won't be able to emerge from the global crisis by ourselves. All the solutions we have been familiar with until today, and all the solutions we are yet to invent, will not help.

From this point onward, our intelligence, our emotions, and the experience we have accumulated won't help us. We have reached a dead end, a total and all-inclusive standstill—an exhaustion of the egoistic desire.

From now on, only the global desire dominates, and we don't know how to handle a global desire. If I am dependent on you, and you are dependent on me, and all of us are dependent on everyone, we have a problem with no solution. Eventually, we might destroy each other.

In the global reality that has been revealed, we need help and new knowledge if we are to survive and continue to develop. This is why the wisdom of Kabbalah is being revealed today.

> *"Open these books and you will find all the good comportments to appear at the end of days. From them you will find the good lesson by which to arrange mundane matters today, as well."*
>
> **Baal HaSulam,**
> *The Writings of the Last Generation*

EVERYONE WILL FEEL IT

Throughout history, we've been in contrast with our root, opposite the Creator, because our nature is egoistic, whereas the Creator's nature is one of love and giving. However, because our egos were small, that opposition didn't cause us much pain. We had problems and hardships, but they weren't of such global dimensions as they are today. Now, our ego has grown to its final degree and has become a single global ego. This is why each and every one of us suddenly experiences much more pain.

Let's explain the matter in a little more depth.

Light spreads from the Creator and traverses all "the Upper Worlds." The worlds are a chain of concealments, a chain of filters diminishing the Light. Finally, only a tiny spark of the Light reaches us. When we are egoistic, dissimilar to the Light, we suffer according to the size of the gap between the spark of Light and our ego.

Until now, each of us was an individual egoist, a separate unit contrary to the Light. This is why the suffering wasn't so terrible. We pacified ourselves thinking that everyone suffers, that's life, we need to get on with it and make ends meet. But now we've entered a new stage: we're in the global world. What's the difference? Simple: now we are all connected.

Henceforth, everyone will increasingly feel the whole of our oppositeness from the Light. Each of us will experience pain, emptiness, and discomfort in life. This is the Law of Existence of the complete system being revealed. Yet, specifically, such a strong degree of oppositeness leads to the beginning of the process of equivalence with the Light.

> "World peace and the knowledge of God are one
> and the same thing."
>
> Baal HaSulam, "The Peace"

EVERYTHING IN GIANT SIZE

In a global world, each act induces a global consequence. A perfect example of a global system is the human body. Each organ has a role within the framework of the body's general functioning. A slight blockage in any tube is enough to cause a chain of damages. Try to recall a time when you had a seemingly minor problem, say in your toenail. How did it affect your overall feeling in your body?

We can learn from that example just how powerful people's actions are in a global world. In such a system, it is possible to lose big time, or win big time. Where else could you find a bank that would give you a seven billion "percent" interest on each investment?

THE FUTURE OF THE HUMAN RACE

Even if we still don't sense the significance of the global world we have entered, the intensity of the ties between us is bound to surface soon.

For now, we can think of it this way: Each of us in the world is holding everyone else's oxygen valve. If anyone doesn't open the valve for me, I won't have any air. This example applies to us all.

What determines whether people will open or close the valves is their attitude toward me. I can't force them to open it; only love will make them do it. In such a world, we won't be able to survive without mutual care.

SHORTAGE OR ABUNDANCE

If we are united in love and mutual concern, the world will be full of abundance and no one will ever lack anything. This is because shortage or abundance results from the way we have adapted to the Upper Light descending to our world.

The consequences of our congruence with the Light or lack of it manifests on all levels of Nature—inanimate (still), vegetative, animate, and human.

Earthquakes, hurricanes, floods, fires, along with problems of depression, dysfunctional families, and the collapse of the global economy all stem from a lack of our congruence with the Light.

It turns out that controlling the world's situation is in our hands.

The Speaking Degree

BOUNDLESS EXISTENCE

We have been developing for generations, and by now we are somewhat satiated. Questions concerning the meaning of existence arise in many people, who find it virtually impossible to continue living aimlessly without knowing life's purpose. Vacations, hobbies, and the rest of life's treats are very nice, but something is still missing.

Kabbalah teaches us that just as there are the still, vegetative, animate, and speaking levels in the evolution of Nature, the same degrees also exist in the human race. Everything we went through until now is part of the development of the human race on the still, vegetative, and animate levels, while today we are at the start of the speaking degree, a completely new level.

In the still, vegetative, and animate degrees, we lived within ourselves. Of course, we also felt others, but they were seemingly in the background, there to serve us. We approached them or distanced ourselves from them according to how our egos assessed the situation, even if we weren't aware of it.

At the speaking degree, we live in unity with others. This brings us a completely different perception of reality, turning man into a truly new creature. We begin to feel life not within us but outside of us. In that state, life won't be limited to several decades. We are meant to ascend to that spiritual level—the speaking degree—during our lifetime in this world. Then, even when our animate body ceases to exist, our spiritual existence will continue.

> *"Spirituality depends on neither time nor place, and there is no death there."*
>
> Baal HaSulam, *The Writings of Baal HaSulam*, "From within my Flesh shall I see God"

THE COLLECTIVE SOUL

Every cell in our body exists only to enable life for the entire body. No cell or organ in the body thinks of itself.

Each of the body's organs operates only to provide the body's needs, and because of it the body is alive.

If we connect among us like cells in a body, with conscious awareness, we'll begin to feel the life of the "collective body" we all share. The system of connections we will build among us will be called "the collective soul," and in it we will feel the spiritual life.

FROM A VIRTUAL CONNECTION TO A SPIRITUAL CONNECTION

Question: It seems to me that people prefer to communicate by e-mail and text messages rather than talking to each other. Why is this so?

It is happening because the ego has developed to such a degree that we prefer a more virtual connection with others. It's not that we don't want the others, but we feel more comfortable when we communicate via text messages or a computer screen. This way we have no contact with each others' bodies or their external forms, and we prefer it this way.

To understand why it happens, we need to know the root of the phenomenon. The will to receive developed in us, and wants to rise above the animate degree, the degree of the body. The animate degree doesn't offer us anything anymore; it doesn't provide us any contact with others.

We seek a more internal connection with others, and in the meantime we've shifted to a virtual connection. This explains the revolution created by the Internet, and why everyone is so drawn to it and to social media. Although the social networks and forums are usually full of nonsense these days, and certainly don't provide any real fulfillment in that connection, it is a certain level of connection after all, and we become addicted to it.

At the next level, the virtual connection won't satisfy us and we will want an even deeper connection. We will feel the need to connect with others internally, at the speaking degree.

THE PEAK OF EVOLUTION

It is Nature's plan to lead its highest degree, the human race, to the maximum development, so the awareness of "Who am I?" "What am I?" "Why, where, how, what for?" grows in us. This is the peak of evolution to which everything from the dawn of Creation is directed.

When we develop the speaking degree within us, we attain everything that happens in Nature and reveal the comprehensive plan of development. We become like the force surrounding all of Nature, and we control all that is taking place in Nature with our feeling, understanding, and knowledge.

> *"The purpose of creation does not apply to the still and the great spheres, such as the earth, the moon, or the sun...nor to the vegetative or the animate... Rather humankind alone ... after they invert their will to receive to a will to bestow, and come to equivalence of form with their Maker, receive all the degrees that have been prepared for them in the Upper Worlds."*
>
> **Baal HaSulam,**
> **"Introduction to the Book of Zohar," Item 39**

SIX THOUSAND YEARS

Approximately 5,774 years ago, the first human being ascended to the speaking degree. The numerous generations living before him had lived without spiritual awareness. He was the first to develop the desire to attain what lies beyond the boundaries of this world.

His name was Adam, from the words *Adame LaElyon*[5] (I will resemble the Most High), and he represented man's desire to resemble the Creator. He was the first Kabbalist, and the first Kabbalistic book, *Angel Raziel*, is attributed to him. The meaning of the title is "The concealed force," relating to the comprehensive force of Nature that governs us but is concealed from us.

The day Adam began to reveal the Creator is called "The day of the creation of the world." This is when humanity touched the spiritual world for the first time, which is why it is the point at which the Hebrew calendar began. According to Nature's plan, within six thousand years at most, all people must climb to the speaking degree.[6]

> *"The whole of humanity is obligated to eventually come to this immense evolvement."*
>
> Baal HaSulam,
> "The Essence of the Wisdom of Kabbalah"

INFINITY–BOUNDLESSNESS

We live in a single reality that appears to be divided into two parts: revealed and concealed. The revealed part is felt by the five senses with which we were born. The concealed part can be revealed only when we correct our desires toward others.

There are degrees of perception in revealing the concealed part. That gradual process can be compared to a person who sees almost nothing without his glasses, but sees just fine with his glasses; he can see far away with binoculars, and with a telescope he can observe the stars. All these instruments improve his vision.

Similarly, we can improve our perception of reality, which is currently concealed, by increasing the correction of our vessels of perception, our desires. Each additional correction further reveals reality to us. This is how the concealed becomes revealed.

When we reveal the entire reality, it is considered that we have gone back to *Adam HaRishon*, to *Ein Sof* [infinity]. What is *Ein Sof*? It is boundlessness, where everything is open before us. All our desires are one hundred percent corrected and full of the Light of *Ein Sof*.

> *"These names, 'revealed' and 'concealed,' are not permanent names, applying to a certain kind of knowledge, as the uneducated think. Rather, they apply only to the human consciousness. Meaning, all those concepts one has already discovered and has come to know through actual experience, man calls 'revealed,' and all the concepts that are yet to be recognized in this manner, man calls 'concealed.'"*
>
> **Baal HaSulam, "Body and Soul"**

Parents, Children, and Education

A NEW GENERATION

Today's generation is a very special one. The things we have become accustomed to pursue don't appeal to the younger generation. They subconsciously feel that our lifestyle won't satisfy them, and that it is not a goal worth living for.

They have new desires, which we cannot restrain. These children seem hyperactive to us, so we give them Ritalin, not realizing that their restlessness is not a disease. It is a natural process of the growth of the ego, which demands a new method of fulfillment. Today's youth can't be satisfied with what satisfied us. They need an upgrade, a new method of education, another life.

Each generation carries within it accumulated impressions from everything that previous generations experienced. That is how it's always been. But today we are at a historical turning point regarding all of human development. We are on the verge of ascending to life on a higher plane. This is why this generation is already filled with the awareness that living as we do now means to waste life. It's as if they've already been through it and don't want to go through it again.

AN INNER VOID

Today's children are born with an inherent need to grasp the meaning of life. That unfulfilled need creates a void within them, which is why it seems as if they don't know what to do with themselves. They look at us grownups with disdain because we can't give them what they need. In fact, even *they* don't know what they want, and certainly can't express it clearly. However, this doesn't change the fact that the emptiness remains.

For lack of any other options, they turn to drugs and alcohol. They aren't to blame; the inner void in them is so vast that they must fill it with something. This is what they are trying to do so they can carry on with life, and this is the root of the global crisis in education.

In this situation, providing them with slightly better education won't help, nor will more sophisticated games. Nothing will satisfy them but the answer to the fundamental question: "Why are we alive?" As parents, we must understand what our children lack. At their deepest level, they are manifesting to us their passion to break through the boundaries of this world.

KNOWLEDGE IS NOT THE SAME AS EDUCATION

Unfortunately, the educational system does not actually engage in "education." It provides children with a certain amount of knowledge in reading and writing, physics, chemistry, and history, but it doesn't educate them or make human beings out of them. The results speak for themselves.

This is clear to anyone who takes a close look at the curriculum. How much time is devoted to discussion and dialogue? What means do teachers use in order to educate? Everything is measured by the amount of knowledge that has been instilled in children's brains, and that's it. It's an industry of grades. Our children turn into robots that know how to carry out certain professional tasks, and are thus fresh blood for the job market, which is controlled by politicians and the financial elite.

The school's primary concern is to "produce" a person who knows how to execute things, to be an engineer, a worker, anything. But nobody cares about the person performing the tasks. That stems from the fact that the current modus operandi of schools evolved during the Industrial Revolution. Schools addressed a need to turn farmers into workers, to teach them basic literacy, mathematics, and engineering so they would know how to operate machines and read instructions. Unfortunately, schools are still governed by that approach.

But now, we've reached a stage where we must shift to a system that actually educates. This has nothing to do with how much a child knows about this or that topic; it is concerned with the extent to which a child grows up to be "human," and being "human" means to unite with others.

THE FUTURE SCHOOL

"We innovate nothing. Our work is only to illuminate what is hidden within man."
Rabbi Menachem Mendel of Kotzk

We need to turn school into a place where children pass time pleasantly because a human being can't develop through oppression. When one is oppressed, he or she closes in and shrinks, and that's exactly what is happening to students today. Children need freedom in order to develop. They have to find their place in the world and their destinations by themselves, and these decisions must come from within them.

THE SOUL IS AGELESS

We should treat children as adults. Children don't need our mushy behavior toward them. Rather, they want to feel that they are like us. Although they are children physically, inside they are adults, and they have adult eyes that look out at us.

When we take a child somewhere, we should explain where we are going, why, and what we will do there. We should consult with them and treat them as adults. If we behave that way, it will bring children immense joy. Indeed, for them, "being adults" is the most joyful game there is!

A NEW WORLD, NEW PATTERNS

At every given moment, both children and adults operate according to thought and behavior patterns they previously saw in their lives. Their manner of behavior, style of speech, dress, and everything else is determined by what they see in others. It begins with Mom and Dad, then with close friends, TV, the Internet, and so forth.

In every situation in life, we imitate behavior patterns that we saw before. We pull out a specific pattern from our "patterns bank" and act it out, just like actors in the theater.

Nowadays, in the new reality in which we are all interconnected, we need to nourish people with a new perspective: world peace is my peace; the world's success is my success. Those are the behavior and education patterns in the new world.

Love Your Friend as Yourself

ABUNDANCE

Today more and more people are falling into depression and despair, escaping to drugs, alcohol, tranquilizers, and the like. It is an unprecedented world phenomenon that is occurring because of rampant dissatisfaction.

What does this lack of satisfaction stem from? It arises from the fact that the desire for pleasure continuously increases, demanding more and more fulfillments that we cannot provide. Hence, we remain empty. The emptiness is felt inside us like a physical hunger. Indeed, dissatisfaction is the darkness of the 21st century.

The wisdom of Kabbalah offers a solution to this helplessness. It explains that there is no direct way to fill the desire for pleasure, so we must rise to another level of fulfillment. We can find pleasure in a type of fulfillment that is always available to us—that of love and bestowal.

There are two opposites here: Precisely when I attain the love of others, I become free. Why? Because I can always love the others and bestow upon them. No one limits me in that. In such a state, I can continually derive pleasure from my actions.

This brings up the question, "Suppose I really want to love others and to give to them, will I have anything to give? After all, I hardly provide for my own needs, let alone those of others."

Indeed, Kabbalists (people who have already gone through the process of emerging from self-love to the love of others), say that the moment we begin to love and bestow upon others, we become filled with abundance from above, the Light of the Creator, which we can transfer to others boundlessly.

In that spiritual state, pleasure fills us, since we desire to thus fill the others. We are immersed in true goodness, which is boundless, and our whole concern is to bestow unto others. Our actions become similar to the Creator's; we become His partners in His actions, in creation, and like Him, we enjoy wholeness and eternity, the highest possible feeling in reality.

Here we can begin to understand that "Love your friend as yourself" is not just a naïve slogan that speaks of being courteous. Rather, it is a means, a lever, a springboard with which to leap to the Creator's degree.

> *"When one comes to love others, he is in direct Dvekut [adhesion], which is equivalence of form with the Maker. Along with it, man passes from his narrow world, filled with pain and impediments, to an eternal and broad world of bestowal upon the Lord and upon people."*
>
> Baal HaSulam,
> "The Essence of Religion and Its Purpose"

LIKE A MOTHER AND CHILD

When a small child wants to eat, drink, play, or take a walk, its mother is at its service. The mother feels the child as an inseparable part of her. More precisely, the child is the key element in the mother's system of desires, hence she gives it her all. That is how Nature causes mothers to treat their offspring in order to sustain the development of life.

To feel the spiritual world, we have to treat others similar to how mothers treat their children. It is a gradual process, and even if it's difficult for us to imagine it as possible—that I should want to fulfill someone else's desire more than my own—still, deep within us, such an attitude exists. There is an inherent spiritual "personality" rooted in us. When we attempt to awaken it through the study of Kabbalah, it comes out of concealment and begins to grow.

RELATING YOURSELF TO THE WHOLE OF CREATION

What do I do if an organ in my body isn't functioning, and I can't make it work? I look for indirect ways to restore it to normal function. When the part has been fixed, it's as if I have reacquired it.

This is how we work with "Love your friend as yourself." We attribute all of Creation to ourselves, returning all its parts to us. We aren't really working toward someone else, but rather learn how to properly treat the parts that are later revealed as our very own.

> *"All you need is to gather all those dwindled*
> *organs that have fallen from your soul, and join*
> *them into a single body. Within that body ...*
> *the fountain of great intelligence and sublime*
> *streams of Light will be as a never ending*
> *fountain, and any place on which you cast your*
> *eyes will be blessed.*
>
> Baal HaSulam, Letter No. 4

ONE LAW

Imagine seven million people being in a state of love, unity, and *Arvut* (mutual guarantee). You don't need to look for guarantors to get a bank loan, and there's no need to hide anything from others. No one has to watch out for one's possessions or set up boundaries. There's no need to legislate everything, just as we don't need to legislate how mothers should treat their babies. Love directs them naturally. When there is love, there is no need for any other law besides the Law of Love.

It is hard for us to accept how everything could be so simple if we acquired the properties of love and bestowal. We wouldn't need to keep an eye on anyone or mention anything to anyone. Each of us would only look for ways to benefit others, and would receive infinite, spiritual pleasure in return.

> *"When one acquires a second nature, which is the*
> *bestowal unto the others ... we will be liberated*
> *from all the incarcerations of Creation... one finds*
> *oneself roaming free in the Creator's world. And*
> *he is guaranteed that no damage or misfortune*
> *will ever come upon him."*
>
> Baal HaSulam,
> "The Essence of Religion and Its Purpose"

Male and Female

TWO OPPOSITES

The big difference between men and women in our world stems from high spiritual roots.

In the spiritual world, the "male" is the giving force, and the "female" is the receiving force. They are two parts of Creation that are equal in their importance, and opposite in their essence. The goal of Creation is for them to unite as one, which Kabbalah terms as "coupling." Yet, even when that happens, the difference between them continues to exist.

MEN, WOMEN, AND LOVE

In our world, everything is dominated by ego, power, and control. In such a world, the status of women seems to be secondary because men naturally have more power, freedom, and independence.

Men are usually physically stronger and occupy places they don't necessarily deserve, and they make most of the decisions. In many cases, women treat them just like mothers treat children, forgivingly moving aside to make room for them. This is how the world operates, unjustly.

The wisdom of Kabbalah speaks of a completely different world, an opposite world in which everything operates according to the force of love and bestowal, which bridges all opposites and differences.

With the shift from an egoistic tendency to one of love and bestowal, we will see a world in which women play a major part, as described in the wisdom of Kabbalah. In the spiritual world, women symbolize the *Sephira Malchut*, which is at the center of Creation. Everything is intended for her, since the birth and blossoming of the new world stem from her.

A SPIRITUAL RELATIONSHIP

"If a man and woman are rewarded, Divinity is between them."

Babylonian Talmud, Suttah, 17a

Couples can take advantage of their relationship for spiritual development if they want to feel the force of bonding—the Creator—in everything that happens between them, and if they intend that He will unite them as one.

In a spiritual relationship between a man and a woman, the couple has a mutual desire to discover the Creator. Each of them relates to the other as a partner the Creator has provided in that process, and they treat the other as a part through which they will realize themselves.

When they try relating to each other through the Creator, they begin to feel that the Creator fills the gaps between them. He comes and binds them, and then their family becomes completely different, a family out of this world.

BEING A MAN

In spirituality, one who nullifies himself is considered a man. It is contrary to the macho image of our world that honors those who dominate and boss everyone around. In spirituality, masculinity is not about overcoming others, but overcoming yourself, your own nature, to make room for the correcting Light to act upon you.

CONCERNING PLEASURE, LIGHT, AND VESSEL

Question: Why are people so attracted to sex?

In the spiritual world, the soul is in a state of "coupling" with the Light. It is a bond between the two parts of Creation, the female side and the male side, and it causes a sense of the most intense pleasure in reality. Physical coupling in the material world represents spiritual coupling. This is also why sex is considered the root of all desires in our world, and so preoccupies us.

The pleasure from sex in our world clearly illustrates the difference between corporeal pleasure and spiritual pleasure. People think so much about sex and imagine the intense pleasure ahead, but when the climactic moment—the moment of satisfaction—finally comes, the pleasure dissipates and disappears almost immediately. Then, the chase begins for the next pleasure.

Spiritual coupling, on the other hand, is an incessant coupling that constantly grows more powerful, giving people a feeling of eternal life. Subconsciously, from within the soul, we all aspire only to that coupling, for this is why we were created.

Deficiency and Fulfillment

MY HEART IS EMPTY

Question: People have many desires and aspirations. They run around, work, advance, and succeed. But why is it that even when we satisfy great desires we feel empty, devoid of meaning?

The wisdom of Kabbalah teaches us that everything the Light (the Creator) created is the desire for pleasure. So there are only two elements in Creation: Light and desire, fulfillment and lack of it, or in simpler terms—pleasure, and the desire for pleasure.

From the initial state called "the eternal world," the created desire cascaded down to this world where it began to develop in degrees—still, vegetative, animate, and human.

Man has desires that are considered "physical desires," like the desire for food, sex, and family, along with "human desires," such as the desire for money, honor, control, and knowledge. The human desires come to us from our surroundings, and we develop through them.

At the end of the development of man's desires, people start to feel emptiness. But Even before that, we feel a certain sense of lack, such as concerning money. Then, once achieved, we turn toward receiving respect. From respect, we move to seeking power, and from power to knowledge. This is how we leap from desire to desire.

Now that the human race has actualized all those desires in general, each according to the extent to which he or she was meant to actualize them—based on the root of one's soul—a new desire is emerging in us, a spiritual one. We don't quite understand the nature of that desire; we only feel that despite all the pleasures this world can offer us, our hearts are still empty. Why are they empty? The things around us no longer satisfy us, and what's ahead remains obscure and concealed.

It is a widespread feeling, which means we have reached a new state: a spiritual desire is awakening within us in order to continue our growth and elevate us back to the root of pleasure—the world of *Ein Sof* (infinity).

IS THERE AN END TO EVIL?

The evil we feel in our world is a force that pushes us to perfect goodness.

As mentioned above, we are made of a desire for pleasure that constantly wants to satisfy itself. For this desire to develop, one is directed to it, as if being told, "You can be fulfilled there," and the desire goes in that direction and fulfills itself. However, the moment the desire has been fulfilled, it is neutralized.

Let's look at our own lives. If we have no desire for anything, we fall into despair. We must desire something, or chase something in order to feel we're alive, in motion. Yet, once we have obtained that filling, the pleasure dissipates and we are left feeling empty. That is how we develop, from chase to chase, moment by moment and generation by generation.

When our development in this world becomes satiated, we begin to feel that nothing in this world can actually fulfill us. At that point we have to advance to a higher world. It turns out that all the bad felt in this world was meant to familiarize us with a different type of filling, one that doesn't dissipate upon fulfillment—an eternal, spiritual fulfillment.

*"One cannot live without vitality and pleasure,
since it stems from the root of creation, which is
His desire to do good to His creatures. Hence,
every creature cannot exist without vitality and
pleasure. Therefore, every creature must go and
look for a place from which it can receive delight
and pleasure."*

Baal HaSulam, *Shamati*, essay no. 35

WHAT'S THE POINT?

More and more people feel that their routine lives aren't satisfying: studying, marrying, buying a car, an apartment, raising children, buying another car, a larger apartment, promotion at work. Many people simply don't want to marry anymore, and out of those that do marry, many divorce because they find no purpose in living together. People have become increasingly self-centered, and it is difficult for them to bear one another and commit themselves; they can barely stand themselves.

Today's life offers a great deal of options for escape: trips, movies, there's always something to do other than think about the meaning of life. Yet, behind those distractions, the nagging question, "What's the point?" still stands.

Go to university, take out a twenty-year mortgage, raise kids ... what for? Only to reach the age of fifty and start caring for the grandchildren and then, at best, they will care for me when I'm in an old-age home, until I go, as well..."

> *"If we were to collect all the pleasures one feels during his seventy years of life and put it on one side, and collect all the pain and sorrow one feels on the other side, if we could see the outcome, we would prefer not to have been born at all."*
>
> **Baal HaSulam, "Peace in the World"**

A NEW METHOD

> *"This world is created with a want and emptiness of all the good abundance, and to acquire possessions we need movement. It is known that profusion of movement pains man... However, it is also impossible to remain devoid of possessions and good... Hence, we choose the torment of movement in order to acquire the fulfillment of possessions. However, because all their possessions are for themselves alone, and 'he who has a hundred wants two hundred,' one finally dies with less than 'half one's desire in one's hand.' In the end, they suffer from both sides: from the pain of*

increased motion, and from the pain of deficiency
of possessions, half of which they lack."
Baal HaSulam, *The Study of Ten Sephirot*,
Part 1, "Inner Reflection," item 21

Throughout history, there were people who reached the conclusion that nothing in our world could completely fulfill humankind. Out of their developed egos, out of the empty chasm within them they discovered a new method to fulfill the desire for pleasure.

These people, beginning with Adam and Abraham, through Moses, Rabbi Shimon Bar-Yochai and The Holy ARI, up to the greatest Kabbalist in our generation, Baal HaSulam, developed the method of Kabbalah for all of us.

Today, when emptiness is "in the air," Kabbalah is being revealed in order to open up a new level of fulfillment with boundless pleasure for us all.

Nature

A TENDENCY TO CONNECT

No part of our body can exist without the other parts. The heart, for example, is a vital part, but what good is it without the brain, the kidneys, the liver, or the lungs?

When the living body developed into its current form, it was as if the various organs reached mutual guarantee. Each organ took a certain role upon itself and delegated the care for the rest of its needs to the other organs. It's as if the heart said, "I will be the pump and leave all the other functions to you. I trust you and give myself to you."

When life first began, there were terrible wars among the cells. Then cells united into cell colonies to defend against the hostile environment, to survive in it, and to get more out of it. Later, within these colonies, they began to divide into different functions. That process already required trust and mutual love because when you give yourself to others, you are totally dependent on them.

Nature's tendency to join individual elements in order to attain further development has now reached the human degree. Such unity doesn't cancel out the uniqueness of each individual. On the contrary, each person finds his or her unique place. Furthermore, unity provides each of us with a new sensation that we could not have felt on our own: that of harmonious life in a higher dimension—the life of the collective body.

> *"When humankind achieves its goal...by bringing them to the degree of complete love of others, all the bodies in the world will unite into a single body and a single heart – only then will all the happiness intended for humanity become revealed in all its glory.*
>
> **Baal HaSulam, "The Freedom"**

ECOLOGY AND NATURAL DISASTERS

The threatening ecological situation has brought about numerous efforts in search of ways to protect Nature. For example, we think that if we burn less fossil fuels, the ecological situation will improve. Thus, we are trying to enforce this limitation through international agreements. But any volcano that erupts emits much more soot and CO_2 than all of our cars combined.

The wisdom of Kabbalah explains that our efforts are currently not directed to the right solution. The lack of balance in Nature stems from a much higher level of obstruction than car emissions or overproduction of plastic. Even if we forced all people to stop polluting the air, it wouldn't restore Nature's balance. The real problem is the level of our thoughts toward others: within us, a volcano is erupting and a tsunami of the ego is destroying everything.

The lack of balance in human relations is increasing daily. It's projected from us to all of Nature's lower degrees—the animate, the vegetative, and the still—resulting in natural disasters that come back to us.

According to Kabbalah, the whole of Nature is one living body, governed by an Upper Thought of love and giving. That Thought governs the universe with perfection at the degrees of still, vegetative, and animate. At the human degree, we have to achieve harmony by ourselves. Until we correct our egoistic hearts and minds, and our relationships with other human beings, the ecological situation will keep worsening and plagues and natural disasters will attack us from all directions.

> *"All sides of reality, their ascents and descents,*
> *depend on the ascent and descent of Man's power*
> *of thought."*
>
> The Raiah Kook, *Treasures of the Raiah*, 1st Ed, p 25

TIME TO UPGRADE

In previous generations, farmers had to consider a few simple situations: when it rained, when it was sunny, when they should sow, and when they should reap. Over time, the demands upon them became more complicated, and they had to become more sophisticated. Today, everything is calculated to the tiniest details—how many drops of water each plant needs, how often to water them, which fertilizer to use, and when to fertilize. Without such precise calculations, the earth wouldn't yield enough.

A similar process should now take place in our human society. Until now, we've been living as we always have. Now we must take more complicated details into consideration in order to survive. It is impossible to continue as we have until now because Nature is demanding that we upgrade our interrelations. We have to learn the rght conditions for raising a new human being, who can prosper in the new world.

CANCER

Today, it seems as if humanity is simply consuming itself: violence, terror, fraud, corruption—people are exploiting each other, and generally behaving like cancerous cells in the body, devouring everything around them. Eventually, that process leads to the consumption of the entire body, including the cancer.

In his essay, "The Peace," Baal HaSulam talks about the "necessity to practice caution with the laws of Nature." He writes, "It is vitally important for us to examine nature's commandments, to know what it demands of us, lest it would mercilessly punish us. We have said that Nature obligates humankind to lead a social life, and this is simple. But we need to examine the commandments that Nature obliges us to keep with respect to the social life.

"In general examination, we find that there are only two commandments to follow in society. These can be called 'reception' and 'bestowal'... We need not excessively examine the commandment of reception, since the punishment is carried out immediately, which prevents any neglect. But in the other commandment, that of bestowal upon society, not only is the punishment not immediate, but it is given indirectly. Therefore, this commandment is not properly observed.

"Thus, humanity is being fried in a heinous turmoil, and strife and famine and their consequences have not ceased thus far. And the wonder about it is that Nature, like a skillful judge, punishes us according to our development. For we can see that to the extent that humankind develops, the pains and torments surrounding our sustenance and existence also multiply.

"Thus you have a scientific, empirical basis that His Providence has commanded us to keep with all our might the commandment of bestowal upon others in utter precision, in such a way that no member from among us would work any less than the measure required to secure the happiness of society and its success. As long as we are idle performing it to the fullest, Nature will not stop punishing us or taking its revenge. And besides the blows we suffer today, we must also consider the drawn sword for the future. The right conclusion must be drawn—that Nature will ultimately defeat us."[7]

LETTING OFF STEAM

We mistakenly think that we are above Nature. It seems to us that Nature is spread out before us, and we need only choose what we want to do with it, as if we really were superior to it. We forget that we also developed from Nature; we didn't just pop up out of the blue. When we understand that we are part of Nature, everything becomes much simpler and we can advance.

The still, vegetative, animate, and human are bound together in a single system that constantly develops. Nowadays, we are required to develop to the next degree of our existence, the development of the human spirit. Our delay in carrying it out creates pressure downward, toward the lower degrees of Nature, like a block in a pipe.

The result is outbursts, and the beginning of these is evident in the still degree: movements of the crust of the Earth, earthquakes, and tsunamis. However, these outbursts could certainly reach higher degrees in the vegetative and the animate.

PROZAC FOR PETS

*"We must not ponder the state of other beings
in the world but man, since man is the center of
Creation. All other creatures...rise and fall
with him."*

**Baal HaSulam,
"Introduction to the Book of Zohar," Item 18**

These days, we are witnessing a new and troubling phenomenon: even our pets are becoming depressed. The manufacture of pet antidepressants is already abundant, and veterinarians are forced to prescribe them more and more often.

That phenomenon shows us how we humans are dragging down the animate world into the human crisis. We are behind, as far as the plan of development that was programmed for us is concerned. We are engaged in petty, superficial things while the rest of Nature is waiting for us to rise to a higher level, and thus elevate all of Creation along with us.

Israel

WE WERE BORN FROM LOVE

"At the age of forty, Abraham came to know his Maker...He began to call out to the whole world. He would walk and call out, gathering the people from town to town and from kingdom to kingdom...Finally, thousands assembled, and they are the people of the house of Abraham. He instilled this great tenet in their hearts, and composed books about it... And the notion was growing and intensifying among the sons of Jacob and their company. Thus, a nation that knew the Creator was born in the world."

**Maimonides, *Mishneh Torah*,
"Laws of Idolatry", 11-16**

If we want to be a unified nation, with a common goal and general mutual consideration, we can use only one method—the method that turned us into a nation in the past. We originated as a group of people with a spiritual goal, created by Abraham. After Abraham developed the method to reveal the Creator, he invited the inhabitants of ancient Babel to study his method, Kabbalah. Thus formed a group of people who learned how to rise above the ego and reveal the Creator among them, the Force of love and giving. In time, that group of Kabbalists was named "the nation of Israel," after its passion to go *Yasher* [straight]-*El* [God], straight to the revelation of the Creator.

No other nation was born out of the principle of love and unity among people. This is the entire life of the nation of Israel, the law of its existence. It is the purpose for which it came into being, and it is why we cannot live any other way. As soon as the Force gluing us together "as one man with one heart" disappeared, we stopped being a nation. As a result, the Temple was ruined and we were exiled.

Likewise, these days we can see that lacking this single uniting principle is the reason why we don't feel like a nation. People don't care about each other, and many Israelis look for ways to run elsewhere. Every once in awhile we unite, but it is only when common problems threaten us from outside. When they pressure us, we unite in order to survive. However, were it not for these problems, we would have devoured each other long ago.[8]

We don't have a natural national bond, such as exists in other nations. Our bond is a spiritual one, and when we lose it, we can't be united; we're not a nation anymore. It turns out that to be established here, we need a method enabling us to actualize the Law of Existence of the Nation of Israel: "Love your friend as yourself."

ABOVE ALL GAPS

"As long as we do not elevate our goal above the corporeal life, we will have no corporeal revival... for we are the children of the idea."

Baal HaSulam, "Exile and Redemption"

The wisdom of Kabbalah explains that a common denominator can't be found on the corporeal level. In our world, everything is divided into infinite pieces. Our common root is only the Creator. Only if we determine that attaining the Creator (the attribute of love and giving) is the goal of our lives will we be able to bridge all the gaps between us.

The wisdom of Kabbalah succeeds in uniting very different people because it ignores corporeal qualities. It aims at the point in the heart of every individual and develops it. When "the point in the heart" appears in people, every corporeal cover drops away, and a true bond is created because that point cannot be filled by a person on one's own.

THE ORDER OF THE WORLD'S CORRECTION

"The Israeli nation had been constructed as a sort of gateway by which the sparks of purity would shine upon the whole of the human race the world over...so they can understand the pleasantness and tranquility that are found in the kernel of love of others."

Baal HaSulam, "Mutual Guarantee," Item 24

Eventually, all of humanity will actualize the law, "Love your friend as yourself." To make the process of correcting human nature easier, this method of correction was developed among a certain group of people known as "the nation of Israel."

Today, we have to reinstate being a spiritual nation, once again knowing the internality of the Torah, the wisdom of Kabbalah, implementing the method of correction on ourselves and helping the entire world ascend. This is called being "A Light for the nations,"[9] and this is our entire vocation as the chosen nation.

Subconsciously, the world feels that the key to happiness is in our hands, that we have something special we're holding back from everyone. According to the wisdom of Kabbalah, that sensation is the source of anti-Semitism. The longer the correction of the world is delayed, suffering increases, and along with it anti-Semitism increases among the nations.[10]

The Book of Zohar writes harsh words in regard to anti-Semitism and the role of Jews: "Woe unto those people ... They are the ones that make the Torah dry, without any moisture of comprehension and reason ... They do not wish to try to understand the wisdom of Kabbalah. Woe unto them, for by these actions they bring about the existence of poverty, ruin, and robbery, looting, killing, and destructions in the world."[11]

In the "Introduction to the Book of Zohar," Baal HaSulam presents these words and explains: "The reason for their words is ... that when all those who engage in the Torah degrade their own internality and the internality of the Torah, leaving it as though it were redundant in the world ... by these actions they cause all forms of externality in the world overpower all the internal parts in the world. ...In such a generation, all the destructors among the nations of the world raise their heads and wish primarily to destroy and to kill the children of Israel, as our sages say, 'No calamity comes to the world but for Israel.' Now it is upon us ... to correct that dreadful wrong

... And then the Nations of the World will recognize and acknowledge the merit of Israel over them. And they shall keep the words of Isaiah, 'And the people shall take them and bring them to their place: and the house of Israel shall possess them in the land of the Lord.' And also 'And they shall bring your sons in their arms, and your daughters shall be carried on their shoulders.'"[12]

Put simply, the key to changing the state of the world and the negative attitude toward Jews is in the Jews' own hands. The moment they begin to implement the method of correction, anti-Semitism will disappear and even their worst enemies will become their friends.

> *"Now the days are nearing for all to know and recognize that the salvation of Israel and the salvation of the entire world depend only on the appearance of the wisdom of the hidden Light of the internality of the secrets of Torah in a clear language."*
>
> **Rav Raiah Kook, *Letters 1*, 92**

THE TEMPLE

> *"A man's heart should be a Temple ... One should be rewarded with the instilling of Divinity."*
>
> **Rav Baruch Shalom Ashlag (Rabash), *The Writings of Rabash*, Vol. 2, "What Is, 'You Have Given Mighty Ones to the Hands of the Weak,' in the Work"**

"Home" is desire and "Holy" is love and bestowal. If one has a holy desire, a desire to love others and bestow upon them, it is called a "Holy Temple" within him.

In the past, that feeling existed in many people who were connected among them. Then, they realized how to express their spiritual attainment in corporeality, as well. As a result, a Holy Temple was built in the material world, too. Today, we should concentrate on the correction of the hearts of all human beings, hence the method of correction is being revealed in the world.[13]

When all of humanity unites and all parts of the collective soul join together in love, we will reach the most exalted state in reality: "The Third Holy Temple." The Light that will be revealed in us in that state will be the greatest Light there is—the Light of "*Yechida*," Light from the degree of "*Keter*."

JEWS AND THE NATIONS OF THE WORLD

"Saying that it is forbidden to teach Torah to idol worshippers ... means that it is impossible to teach Torah as long as they are still in a state

of idol worshipping, meaning when they are still immersed in self-love."

Rav Baruch Shalom Ashlag (Rabash), *The Writings of Rabash*, Vol. 2,
"What Is, 'It Is Forbidden to Teach
Idol-Worshippers Torah,' in the Work"

"Forbidden," according to the wisdom of Kabbalah, means "impossible." Idol worshipping means that one is still in a state of self-love, bowing down to the ego. "Studying Torah" means revealing the ways by which the Upper Light expands in your *Kelim* [vessels].

Spiritually speaking, every person is initially considered an "idol-worshipper," "nations of the world." Only after one corrects one's ego and becomes similar to the Creator, to the force of love and giving, is one considered a Jew, capable of "studying Torah." A Jew is a spiritual state we must acquire by ourselves. It is not something we are born with. "Jew" (Heb. *Yehudi*) comes from the word, *Yehud* (unity), and it is one who unites with the Creator out of equivalence with Him.[14]

It turns out that initially, we're all nations of the world and can't "study Torah" because we're incapable of revealing the Light. What can we do? This is where the method of correction, Kabbalah, enters the picture.

It enables us to connect with "The Light that reforms," a type of illumination that comes from our corrected state to our present state, according to the intensity of our desire to advance. That illumination gradually purifies us and turns us into Jews, enabling us "to study Torah."[15]

The Vessel
and the Light

FEELING MORE

Question: What is the light that is mentioned in
Kabbalah? Are these actual rays of light?

Light is what fills my emotions and my mind. It is a
feeling, an understanding, a realization. Any filling
is called Light, all types of delight and pleasure are called
"Light." In our present situation, we live in this world
and feel all kinds of pleasures. They are also considered
lights, but very small ones. In the words of *The Zohar*,
they are called "a sliver of light," a tiny spark of light
bringing life to this entire world.

Science also discovered that our universe began with
a spark of unique energy. That was but a spark of spiritual

Light bursting into our world and creating everything in it, including us.

The rest of the Light's intensity is beyond the degree of this world.[16] It can be felt only if we have the same quality as the Light: love and giving. That means there will be no boundaries whatsoever or curtains hiding anything from us.

> *"Prior to emerging from self-love, a person is incapable of feeling the Light. Thus, first one needs to exit self-love. Otherwise the restriction lies over a person."*
>
> Rav Baruch Shalom Ashlag (Rabash), *The Writings of Rabash*, Vol. 1, "One Does Not Pretend to Be a Wicked"

THE FIRST LESSON IN KABBALAH

The "Light" (pleasure) creates the "vessel" (will to receive delight and pleasure). Everything existing in the vessel comes from the Light. There is nothing but the Light and the vessel.

We feel what exists to the extent of our development. When a baby is born, it understands the world to a certain degree. The more it grows, the more it understands. This is also how we grow in spirituality: We develop our *Kli* [vessel] to feel the eternal filling that permanently exists, to reveal the Light in its entirety.

A PASSION FOR THE LIGHT

We all emerged from the Light; this why we eventually want to attain it. All our passions, all our longings are for it. Subconsciously, that's all we desire.

All the pleasures in our lives—new clothes, a nice car, good food, anything—actually stem from the Light. The pleasures appear to us cloaked in specific covers, such as pleasure from rest, warmth, or a scenic view. However, in all of them, we actually feel the Light.

Gradually, we will permeate those covers and we'll want to reveal their source—the Light Itself. I don't really need a shiny car. True, it gives me pleasure, but I want more. I want pleasure even without that piece of metal, which doesn't excite me after a while, anyway.

As we develop, we come to want more subtle things, more covert. Instead of the large, bulky stuff we had in the past, everything has become small, diminished. Quantity is turning into quality.

Similarly, our desires develop from desires for material possessions to desires for spiritual attainment. Within us, we come to discern our longing for the Light. It should fill us in itself, not just through food, sex, money, honor, control, or knowledge.

People don't really understand the process we're going through, or that the lack of Light is behind the depression, despair, addictions, divorces, and violence spreading in our society.

REVEALING THE LIGHT

*Behold that before the emanations were emanated
and the creatures were created, The Upper Simple
Light had filled the whole existence. And there was
no vacancy, such as an empty air, a hollow, but all
was filled with that Simple, Boundless Light.*

*And when upon His simple will, came the desire
to create the worlds and emanate the emanations,
to bring to light the perfection of His deeds, His
names, His appellations, Which was the cause
of the creation of the worlds, Then the Ein Sof
restricted Himself, in His middle point.*

The Ari, *Tree of Life*, Part One, Gate One

The wisdom of Kabbalah teaches us that everything comes from the Light. Within the Light, one small point is created, and from that the entire reality evolves. That point is the substance of Creation. The point begins to expand within the Light, conceal the Light, receive different forms from the Light, and move away from the Light on all different levels and degrees. "Worlds" are created from the point—the disappearance and diminishing of the Light.

The point reaches a state in which a discernment called "man" is created—a desire that understands itself, senses itself, that is about to know who created it. It has a kind of reverse gear toward the Light that created and designed it. It asks "why" and "how." That's how the Light awakens it, but that desire begins to sense itself as independent, existing, returning toward the Light, and building itself.

We can see it in the evolution of life in our world, in how a small body is created from a drop of semen, almost from scratch. Gradually, that body begins its personal development—in desires, thoughts, and in having its own views. This is also how we grow spiritually. That black point that was once formed in the Light begins to understand itself and connect itself to the Light. Eventually, the point becomes like the actual Light.

CONSTANT BESTOWAL

"There is no change in the Light. Rather, all the changes are in the vessels."
Baal HaSulam, *Shamati*, Essay no. 3

The Light is in a state of complete rest, static. It only bestows. It is like a provider to which I can draw near or distance myself.

I can scream to it; it couldn't care less. All my yelling might cause a change within me, in which case I'll feel a different outcome of Its constant bestowal. That is, in the changes I experience I sense It differently, but it is I who senses "It" differently, and not that It is different. Just so, the sun never ceases to shine. I can warm and cool things with its energy, or do whatever I wish, but the energy is constant.

Likewise, the Light is "good and does good" to the good and to the bad. What does that mean "to the good and to the bad"? Is It also good to evildoers? Yes, except they are opposite from It, and suffer according to the extent of their oppositeness, which is what causes them to develop.

THE POINT OF CONNECTION

When people reveal a bond among them above the increasing ego, precisely at that point of connection they feel a unique phenomenon called "Light."

It is a type of supplement connecting them, developing them to the degree of higher understanding and connection. The wisdom of Kabbalah explains that the secret of existence is in the point of connection among people because the same force that bore us, the Light, is hidden among us.

Kabbalah Writings

THE WORLD OF FORCES

Upper forces descend to our world and operate in it. Everything we see in our world, including ourselves, is a result of the activity of those forces. We don't feel the forces themselves or see where they come from because they arrive from a higher world, the world of forces.

The Kabbalists revealed the Upper World and wrote about it. Thus, they enabled us to read about the Upper Forces and how they descend into our world and operate everything. The Kabbalists did that so we could ascend in the same way the forces descend, back to their roots.

The Upper Forces are the opposite of us. We are made of a desire to receive, whereas those forces are desires to bestow and to give.

While reading Kabbalah writings, we should intend for those forces to bestow their quality upon us, to make us similar to them. The reading affects us and we slowly begin to draw near them according to our efforts, just as when children play games, the games cause them to grow and develop.

KABBALISTS WRITE

Question: Why did Kabbalists write books, and what is so special about writing?

Writing is revealing. In every generation, Kabbalists write books because from generation to generation the souls have larger egos and a new perception. The conditions for the revelation of spirituality change and Kabbalists need to update and adapt the method of correction.

In his essay, "The Teaching of Kabbalah and Its Essence," Baal HaSulam explained, "The wisdom of truth, like secular teachings, must be passed on from generation to generation. Each generation adds a link to its former one, and thus the wisdom evolves. Moreover, it becomes more suitable for expansion in the public."

One who develops spiritually and connects to the inner meaning of the text discovers an entire world within them. That person begins to realize that the text is like a system operating upon us. That is, it is not merely a text, but a program that envelopes one who begins to work with one's desire, building them in accord with the Upper system.

To summarize, through writing, the Kabbalist conveys instructions for spiritual development, but also transfers inner strength from the Upper system. This is why reading Kabbalah writings advances people to spirituality.

THE WRITINGS OF BAAL HASULAM

> *"And I have named that commentary The Sulam (Ladder) to show that the purpose of my commentary is as the role of any ladder: if you have an attic filled abundantly, then all you need is a ladder to reach it. Then, all the bounty in the world will be in your hands."*
>
> Baal HaSulam, "Introduction to The Book of Zohar," Item 58

Baal HaSulam did tremendous work in revealing the wisdom of Kabbalah. Without him, we lay people, who don't have special souls like the few chosen Kabbalists of the past, wouldn't be able to attain spirituality.

The power of that great Kabbalist is evident in the way he "set things straight" on all levels. His predecessors attempted to express the entire system of Creation in the language of the Bible, the legends, the law, and Kabbalah. But thanks to him we can study the unfolding of reality in an organized and methodical fashion.

> "My being rewarded with the manner of disclosing the wisdom is because of my generation."
>
> Baal HaSulam, "Teaching of the Kabbalah and Its Essence"

THE FORCE OF THE MESSIAH

> "And the dissemination of the wisdom in the masses is called 'a Shofar [a festive horn].' Like the Shofar, whose voice travels a great distance, the echo of the wisdom will spread throughout the world, so even the nations will hear and acknowledge that there is Godly wisdom in Israel... The generation is worthy of it, as it is the last generation, which stands at the threshold of complete redemption. And for this reason, it is worthy of beginning to hear the voice of Messiah's Shofar, which is the revealing of the secrets."
>
> Baal HaSulam, "Messiah's Shofar [horn]"

The force that draws us from self-love to love of others is called the "Messiah." The force of the Messiah must be revealed within each and every individual and correct the egoism imbued in all of us from birth. This is why the Kabbalah writings have been revealed to the world in our generation.

In Kabbalah, the force of the Messiah is also called "The Light that reforms." So instead of waiting for some great leader to come and perform miracles and wonders, it's better to open the Kabbalah writings and learn how to cause that Light to operate on us.

The Study of Kabbalah

NO PREREQUISITES

Question: Can anyone study Kabbalah, even without proficiency in the Bible?

There is no need for any preliminary knowledge in order to study Kabbalah. The Torah of Truth, meaning the internality of Torah, which is the wisdom of Kabbalah, sets no prerequisites for anyone. Everyone may study.

Even if someone is illiterate and only listens to Kabbalah lessons, listening alone works. Eventually, that person will begin to feel the truth. In the Torah of Truth, we don't advance through our intellect, but through the will to develop spiritually. Particularly among people who understand less of the learned material, and are frustrated and thus feel deficient, the new vessels of feeling can open even faster.

A HEALING FORCE

"Why then did the Kabbalists obligate each person to study the wisdom of Kabbalah? Indeed, there is a great thing in it, worthy of being publicized: There is a wonderful, invaluable remedy to those who engage in the wisdom of Kabbalah. Although they do not understand what they are learning, through the yearning and the great desire to understand what they are learning, they awaken upon themselves the Lights that surround their souls."

Baal HaSulam,
"Introduction to the Study of the Ten Sephirot,"
Item 155

When we read in the Kabbalistic writings that we should anticipate "The Light that reforms," to what can that be compared? It is like a sick person getting an intravenous infusion. With each drop, more of the medication enters the veins. Likewise, with each and every word, we should anticipate the Light that reforms.

At first, we don't know exactly what Light is and how It reforms. We also don't really know the good to which we should aspire. Still, the main thing is to anticipate the remedy from studying.

Kabbalah writings enable us to connect to a power source from a different dimension. Through the writings, an intravenous infusion drips into us from the Upper World, returning us to spiritual life.

SURROUNDING LIGHT

I am in a large, expansive system, which I don't feel or understand. In that tremendous system, I live in a tiny place called "this world."

How do we reveal the entire system, know it all, feel it all, and become its owner? Drawing the Light within the system is the force that will open up my senses, my inner channels, the force of life that will restore my consciousness.

That Light surrounds me in the Upper Reality. It is there this very moment, but I don't feel it because my qualities are opposite from those of the Light. However, I can evoke its influence on me and then that influence is called "Surrounding Light."

The Light surrounds me, caresses me, and nurtures me until I awaken.

> *"Man was created only to study*
> *the wisdom of Kabbalah."*
>
> **The Writings of The Ari,**
> **Rav Chaim Vital's Preface to The Gate to Introductions**

HE WHO DAMAGED US WILL COME TO CORRECT

I cannot rise above my ego with my own strength. Indeed, if my entire being is the egoistic will to receive, surely I won't be able to pull myself out of myself.

This is where the system of correction comes in—the study, books, the teacher, and the group. Through that system I draw to me the Light that reforms—the unique force that affects me and corrects me.

No one is asking me to correct what the Creator spoiled. The Creator has said in that regard: "I have created the evil inclination; I have created the Torah as a spice."[17] I am the One who created you deficient, and I am the One who will correct you. You only need to realize that your inclination is evil, and demand of Me to change it to a good inclination. I am waiting for you."[18]

HOW THE LIGHT OPERATES

The Upper Force of Nature, the force of love and giving, is in the bond between all parts of Creation, which He Himself created, existing in harmony and mutual connection.

We feel bad because we have left that integrated system. If we want to feel good, we need to try to return to that system called "wholeness."

How do we return? When we want to return to the system and exert ourselves, we awaken from within it a force that influences us. This is regarded as "invoking the Light that reforms on ourselves," the Surrounding Light, the force that returns us to the comprehensive system.

That force operates according to the intensity of our desire, to the same extent that we can evoke, request, and demand it from the system.

THE REAL ME

When the Light shines, It opens all kinds of qualities that exist within me. These qualities are concealed from me; I neither see nor feel them.

It seems to me that I am growing, like a baby who has gained some weight and a few inches, but this is not the case. It only seems that way to me, but nothing truly new can be revealed.

I am eternal, except now I am only slightly familiar with myself. I have to draw the Light to continue opening more qualities within me until I return to *Ein Sof* [infinity].

I want qualities that are closer to the Creator's to appear within me, qualities that are more developed. I want to open up, and for the Light to come and increasingly open me.

It turns out that I don't disclose the Light, but draw It so It discloses me—my true self—greater and nearer to *Ein Sof*.

And when I'm further revealed to myself, it is considered that I'm climbing the ladder of degrees.

Imaginary Reality

LIVING IN FANTASY LAND

When we watch a good movie, our impression of it can be so powerful that we'll forget about the outside world. We get carried away with the plot, which becomes our reality. We cry, laugh, love, hate, fear, hope, lose, and win.

According to Kabbalah, our life is one long movie. We sleep, wake up, eat, drink, have children, live, and die—all in that movie. It feels so real because we've never been outside of it. We live in a theater called "this world" until suddenly someone comes and tells us: "Listen, you are in a theater, You are on a trip, some electrodes were implanted in you, and through them images are projected in your brain."

To wake up from the movie, we are given the wisdom of Kabbalah. We don't change anything in life artificially; we only study. While studying, the unique force in the Kabbalistic writings, the Light that reforms, influences us. As we gradually change, so does our perception of reality.

ALL WHO FAULT, FAULT IN THEIR OWN FLAWS

Egoistic tendencies such as control and pride are embedded in all of us. When they arise in us, we don't pay much attention to them, but control and arrogance in other people upset us.

Our ego, like a strict, perceptive judge, helps us investigate the evil that is revealed to us in others. We judge them carefully and deeply, noticing each and every detail.

The ego enables us to identify bad things outside of us first, and only afterwards realize that actually everything is within us. This is what is called, "All who fault, fault in their own flaws."[19] However, we are about to discover that it isn't that "He is bossy" and "She is arrogant," but that it is I who see them as such because of my uncorrected desire.

> "He who sees any evil in his friend, it is like
> looking in the mirror: If his face is filthy, he sees it

in the mirror, too, and if his face is clean, he sees
no flaw in the mirror. As he is, so he sees."

Baal Shem Tov[20]

INTERNAL VESSELS, EXTERNAL VESSELS

We are in a perfect system formed by the Creator. The whole of the substance of Creation is the "will to receive," and the perfect system is actually the collective desire that was created. That desire is also called the "collective soul" or the "soul of *Adam HaRishon* [the first man]." But the Creator shattered the collective soul into numerous particles. Each of us contains but a shattered particle of the collective soul.

Because of the shattering, in our world each one's desire divides into two main parts: internal vessels (*Shoresh* [root], *Neshama* [soul], and *Guf* [body]) and external vessels (*Levush* [robe/clothing] and *Heichal* [hall]).

I feel my internal vessels as "I," myself, so I care about them. I feel my external vessels as strangers, as not mine. The internal and external vessels are contrary to each other—the more I love my internal vessels, the more I hate my external vessels.

Why? The "boundary of the shattering" stands between the two types of vessels like a partition that causes me to look outside. I do this only to see how I can benefit from any situation, and what I can get out of it. This forces me to treat others egoistically, desiring to take advantage of them.

AS THOUGH WE WERE DREAMING

"All generations since the beginning of Creation to the end of correction are as one generation that has extended its life over several thousand years, until it developed and became corrected as it should be."

Baal HaSulam, "The Peace"

Until now, it seemed to us that "I" and "the world" were two separate things. But now, at the end of human development, which has spanned over tens of thousands of years, we are being required to realize that "I" and "the world" are one whole, that Nature really is global, and that all the still, vegetative, animate, and human constitute a single mechanism.

Also, we are nearing the realization that indeed there is no one *outside* of us, but everything takes place *within* us. This is a higher perception of reality. We are about to discover exciting revelations in the Upper Dimension. This is the entrance to the new life, an awakening from the dream we have been living until now, from the illusionary sensation that we are living in a reality that is divided and separated into parts.

When we look back on the past, we'll begin to absorb the fact that the egoistic attitude we had toward everyone around us actually harmed us. We hated ourselves, took advantage of ourselves, lied to ourselves, and stole from ourselves. It will become clear that we simply lived a lie, a grave mistake.

And yet, each such revelation will promote us one more step toward complete unity and harmony with all of reality, which will be revealed to us as being our own selves. Moreover, along with the revelation that we belong to the whole of reality, and vice versa, we will also reveal the Upper Force present in everything—the force of love and giving.

LIKE A RADIO RECEIVER

The Upper Light is around us in complete rest. It is a field of infinite information, of eternity and wholeness. However, we don't feel it because we are closed within ourselves. Our ego encloses us inside.

To feel the Light, we must build within us a quality that is similar to the quality of the Light, a quality of love and giving. This is similar to how a radio receiver creates within it the same wavelength that it wants to receive from the outside.

The wisdom of Kabbalah is actually the wisdom of receiving. It is a scientific method for building a quality that enables us to receive the information existing in the field surrounding us. When we do, we won't feel enclosed within us. Instead, we will be truly flowing in the eternal and whole Upper Light, in the wave of eternity.[21]

SELF-UPGRADE

Suppose I only have the Word program installed on my computer, and I get an Excel or a picture file attached to an e-mail message. I try to open the file using Word, but it doesn't open. There might be something very good for me in that file, but my program refuses to open it. I have no choice but to install a new program on my computer, which will be able to read the data and present them to me. Of course, a new format of data requires a new program.

We go through a similar process in our spiritual development. Using the wisdom of Kabbalah, we acquire a new program, "place" it on our desire, and then we can receive new images, new information. Until now, we had only the original program with which we were born, which is totally directed toward self-love. Now, we are upgrading ourselves, acquiring a program that understands the concept of a love of others. With the new program, the new files we are receiving open just fine!

> *"Self-love is our obstacle to reaching the delight and pleasure."*
>
> Rabash, *The Writings of Rabash*, Vol. 1,
> "Sometimes Spirituality Is Called a 'Soul'"

A NEW QUALITY, A NEW IMAGE

If we had other senses, different ones, we'd sense reality differently. We see it in other animals. Dogs, for example, perceive reality primarily through smell; snakes perceive it through temperature, and bats and dolphins through their hearing. So what is the actual reality? Is there such a thing?

At the start of the twentieth century, Einstein introduced to the world a new concept: The Theory of Relativity. He discovered that changing the speed of the observer (or the observed object) yielded a completely different vision of reality on the axis of space and time. Later, quantum physicists found that man impacts the event he is observing, that the image of reality is actually a kind of average between the qualities of the observer and the qualities of the object or phenomenon being observed.

Since we were born, we have been perceiving reality in a certain way. This is why we think that that's the way reality is. But the truth is that it is all only in our perception. You may ask, "What difference does it make to us? Why do Kabbalists deal with the perception of reality and bother explaining to us that the image of reality is relative and dependent upon us?" They do it because the method of Kabbalah enables us to add new senses to ourselves, new qualities, so we can begin to sense another world through them.

Indeed, we don't know where we came from or where we are headed, and during our short lives we can't really control what happens to us in life, or change our fate for the better. That option exists only in a higher world.

Just like a near-sighted person wearing glasses to identify what exists around him, we can add new qualities to our original nature and see the Upper World through them, from which the Upper Forces descend to our world and govern everything. Our image of the world won't disappear, but will, instead, be added to with a new one.

A MAN LIVES WITHIN HIMSELF

In his "Preface to the Book of Zohar" (item 34), Baal HaSulam writes, "Take our sense of sight, for example: we see a wide world before us, wondrously filled. But in fact, we see all that only in our own interior. In other words, there is a sort of photographic machine in our hindbrain, portraying everything that appears to us and nothing outside of us." He also explains that in our minds there is "a kind of polished mirror that inverts everything seen there, so we will see it outside our brain, in front of us."

To illustrate the matter, let's compare a person to a closed box with five entry channels: eyes, ears, nose, mouth, and hands. Those organs represent the five senses: sight, hearing, smell, taste, and touch, through which a person perceives that which is outside.

Various stimuli enter through these five entry channels, which are gathered and processed according

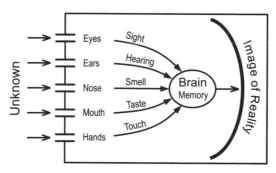

to the information found in the person's memory. The result is an image of reality that is then projected on a "movie screen" in the hindbrain.

It turns out that what we perceive, we perceive within us. The truth is that there's nothing outside of us, we only imagine that there is. Just like in a dream, our eyes are closed and we don't see anything, but we experience all kinds of "movies" in our minds. This also occurs when we are awake and all our senses are active.

Whatever we feel are our internal impressions, *Reshimot*. The way we process the *Reshimot* that float within us at every moment is what determines our image of reality. Naturally, we process egoistically, so we get an image of this egoistic world. But when we process out of the new qualities of loving and giving, we see the image of the spiritual world.

It turns out that we can't count on any positive change coming from the outside; everything depends on our changing our inner qualities.

> *"All the worlds, Upper and lower,*
> *are included in man."*

Baal HaSulam,
"Introduction to the Preface to the Wisdom of Kabbalah," Item 1

BUILDING REALITY

There are two fundamental forces in Nature: the force of receiving and the force of giving. The wisdom of Kabbalah says that different combinations of those forces create all that exists in reality, including us. We sense a world full of colors, sounds, shapes, bodies, and events. All these stem from a certain combination of those two fundamental forces.

Kabbalah enables us to emerge from the image currently projected to us, and become the directors of our own reality. Both forces—the force of receiving and the force of giving—are placed in our hands and we begin to shape them into forms. Step by step, world after world, we create a new image until we achieve the complete reality called "the world of infinity [Ein Sof]."

The Point
in the Heart

INNER COMPASS

Question: Is there a compass within us that
directs us to reveal the spiritual world?

Initially, I was created in my corrected form, in a
state called "the world of *Ein Sof*." I descended from
there and fell into a state called "this world"—the faulty,
opposite state. I am supposed to ascend by exactly the
same way I descended.

When do I begin to feel that I'm ready for the way, and
how do I know what is the way? There is a combination
of two factors here. On the one hand, I suffer in this
life. It's not necessarily physical suffering; I may have
material abundance, but still feel empty. On the other

hand, I feel a certain attraction, tendency, a yearning to attain the origin of life. This is already the awakening of "the point in the heart."

That point is like a spiritual gene implanted in me, a drop of spiritual seed from which my soul will develop. The chain of transitions I will undergo on the way back to *Ein Sof* is defined in "the point in the heart." Then, whether I want to or not, I feel I must reach the solution. Whether I want it or not, I will encounter the wisdom of Kabbalah, wherever I may be on earth. In fact, there are examples that are simply mind-boggling regarding where and how people found Kabbalah.

How does it happen? Our world is a spiritual field, like a magnetic field, and the point in the heart leads us to a place where we may nurture and fill it.

> *"Whoever wants to taste the taste of life should pay attention to his point in the heart."*
> Rabash, *The Writings of Rabash*, Vol. 3, "TANTA"

BORN INVOLUNTARILY

I was born with qualities I didn't choose. Then, the surroundings, my family, and the education I received operated on me from the outside and fashioned me a certain way. This is how I live—a result of those two givens in which I had no say.

Suddenly questions arise in me: "Why am I alive? What for?" I didn't choose those questions either, they simply popped out. This is the beginning of the awakening of the "point in the heart," which draws us to a higher world. Here is where the possibility of free choice begins.

> "A person should have faith that he has a point in the heart, which is the illuminating spark. And we should constantly awaken that spark, because he has the option of igniting his actions, so they illuminate."
>
> Rabash, *The Writings of Rabash*, Vol. 2, "What Is, 'The Herdsmen of Abraham's Cattle and the Herdsmen of Lot's Cattle,' in the Work"

BEGINNING OF THE SOUL

The entire spiritual development occurs in "the point in the heart." We need to develop it and "inflate it" until it's as big as a balloon. In it, we will reveal the Upper Worlds and spiritual life.

The difference between feeling it as a small point and feeling the whole world inside of it depends on our ability to discern. Let's put it this way: From outer space, a city on Earth looks like a dot. The closer we get, the more details we see. We discern buildings, cars, and trees. So the closer we get to an object, the more details we discern.

Our ability to discern details in the point develops along with the work with the Light that reforms, which is found in Kabbalistic writings. It follows that we needn't yearn for some spiritual place "above," but only to expand the point within us. This is the beginning of the soul.

> *When man is born, he immediately has a*
> *Nefesh of Kedusha (Holiness)...which, due to its*
> *smallness, is called a "point." It dresses in man's*
> *heart, in one's will to receive, which is found*
> *primarily in one's heart.*
>
> Baal HaSulam,
> "Introduction to the Book of Zohar," Item 43

A SOURCE OF PLEASURE

If the "point in the heart" hasn't yet awakened in someone, he or she won't feel any connection with what Kabbalah discusses. These matters will seem insignificant. However, once the point has awakened, a person will simply feel, even if he or she can't actually understand the issues, there is something in this wisdom that touches deep inside. Thus, that person will find a source of delight for the soul.

> *"And when the Upper Light shines in the heart,*
> *the heart will strengthen."*
>
> Baal HaSulam, *Shamati*, Essay no. 68

Souls

I AM ETERNAL

No one thinks that life ends with his or her death. Even if they say otherwise, subconsciously, people don't think that way. If we did, we wouldn't have the strength to live even a single moment longer.

In each of us is a spark deep inside, connecting us to eternity. We all sense that our lives are somehow different from those of animals. Even if we're not aware of it, that notion influences our entire approach to life.

DEVELOPING THE SOUL

"The will to receive is imprinted in each creature, and constitutes disparity of form from the Creator, hence the soul parted from Him as an organ that separated from the body ... That clarifies what the Creator wants of us—equivalence of form, for then

we cleave to Him once more ... meaning change
our qualities, the will to receive, and acquire the
qualities of the Creator, which is only to bestow,
so that all our actions will be only to bestow upon
the others and benefit them to the best of our
ability. By that we achieve the goal of cleaving
unto Him, for this is equivalence of form."

Baal HaSulam, *The Writings of the Last Generation*, Part I

Developing the soul means to develop a quality similar to the Creator's, one of bestowal and love. If we acquire that quality then we have become similar to the Creator. Within that quality, we reveal the Creator while living in this world.[22]

CLINICAL DEATH

Question: What does Kabbalah say about phenomena that are sometimes felt during clinical death, of a person exiting the body and seeing it from above?

It is nothing more than a psychological phenomenon. It's not a person who is already inside the soul and observes the body from within it. Although it is a certain detachment from the body, it is nothing more than that. Rather, these are psychosomatic phenomena, not spiritual ones.

It is important to understand that if a person doesn't develop the soul during one's life, he or she won't have a feeling of the spiritual world when passing away, either. That person remains with the same potential point embedded within from birth, and will need to return to this world to develop it next time.

One who did develop the soul, however, will feel both worlds at once. The person feels this world through the five senses, and the spiritual world (a.k.a. "the next world") through the soul. When the body dies and a person ceases to feel this world through the five senses, the soul remains, along with the feeling of the spiritual world.

> *"Man finds in the future only the Light he knowingly drew in this world. He who knew the internality will enjoy the Inner Light, and he who did not attain It will not enjoy It whatsoever."*
>
> The Ramchal,
> in his letter to Rabbi Bassan [in the Book *Yarim Moshe*, [*When Moses Lifted*], Letter no. 62

INCARNATIONS

*"Everyone is born with but a small piece of the
soul of Adam HaRishon. When one corrects that
piece, he no longer needs to reincarnate."*

**Rabash, *The Writings of Rabash*, Vol. 1,
"What Is the Degree One Should Achieve
so He Will Not Have to Reincarnate?"**

The Creator created one soul called *Adam HaRishon*. That soul divided into numerous human souls. If, during this life, a desire for spirituality awakens in a person through the study of Kabbalah, one can reveal the spiritual world and return to the root of the soul in *Adam HaRishon*.

A person who does that during one's lifetime has realized himself or herself. A person who ended life without attaining the root of the soul returns to this world and is born into a new body. This is how things proceed until all the people correct themselves and are re-included in *Adam HaRishon*.

*"Man reincarnates until he merits attaining the
wisdom of the truth to the fullest. Without them,
his soul will not grow to its full degree."*

Baal HaSulam, "From My Flesh Shall I See God"

WHO'S ALREADY THERE?

In principle, when one enters the spiritual world, he or she reveals who is and who isn't in it. However, if a Kabbalist wants to conceal himself, he can't be seen. There are Kabbalists with particular roles who conceal themselves. Conversely, other Kabbalists take the role of receiving the new souls arriving at the spiritual world and familiarizing them with it.

A person who has been rewarded with "opening one's eyes"—the revelation of the spiritual world—meets a "guide" who assists him. The Zohar[23] dedicates a special essay to tell of those unique souls meeting the individual. Such a soul is called "a donkey driver," since it helps a person ascend with one's "donkey"—one's matter (the will to receive)—on the 125 degrees of the spiritual world up to Ein Sof [infinity].

The Book of Zohar

UPPER RADIANCE

*"This book was called The Book of Zohar
[radiance] because of the imparting of that Light
from the Upper Radiance."*

Ramak , *Know the God of Thy Father,* 2

*T*he Book of Zohar is the primary source we have for
the correction of man and the world. Among all
the holy writings ever written, from *Raziel the Angel*
through the Bible and up to our time, no book equals
the spiritual power of *The Book of Zohar*. When it is
said that Kabbalah is "the internality of the Torah" or
"the Torah of truth," it refers first and foremost to *The
Book of Zohar*.

In our generation, *The Zohar* has been revealed to the world thanks to the *Sulam* [ladder] commentary, and thanks to the introductions to *The Zohar* written by Rav Yehuda Ashlag (Baal HaSulam).

The Book of Zohar is a closed system built in a unique way. It seemingly tells us what is happening in our world: stories of people, animals, trees, flowers, mountains, and hills. However, it actually speaks of the soul and the Upper Forces. That system was meant to advance us toward boundless existence in our comprehension and feeling.

Approximately 1,800 years ago, ten Kabbalists of the highest spiritual level joined together and wrote *The Zohar* for us. In that group of Kabbalists were unique souls representing the ten *Sephirot*, the ten foundations of the comprehensive system of Creation. They were able to express the entire structure of reality. At the head, Rabbi Shimon Bar Yochai represented the *Sephira Keter*, and the others with him represented the *Sephirot* [plural of *Sephira*] *Hochma, Bina, Hesed, Gevura, Tifferet, Netzah, Hod, Yesod,* and *Malchut*.

The authors of *The Zohar* used signs called "letters" to express the external form of the system in which they were situated. If we wish to connect to that system through the letters and the words, the system begins to affect us. *The Book of Zohar* can be compared to a touch screen—"touching" *The Zohar* connects us with the comprehensive system of Creation and makes us grow and develop spiritually.

> *"The prohibition from above to refrain from*
> *open study of the wisdom of truth was for a*
> *limited period, until the end of 1490. Thereafter*
> *is considered the last generation, in which the*
> *prohibition was lifted and permission has been*
> *granted to engage in The Book of Zohar. And*
> *since the year 1540, it has been a great Mitzva*
> *(precept) for the masses to study, old and young."*

Rabbi Abraham Ben Mordechai Azulai,
"Introduction to the book, *Ohr HaChama* [*Light of the Sun*]," 81

THE RIGHT APPROACH

> *"This point in time requires accelerated*
> *acquisition of the inner Torah. The Book of Zohar*
> *breaks new paths and makes a highway in the*
> *desert. The Zohar and all its harvest are ready to*
> *open the doors of redemption."*

The Raiah Kook, *Orot* [*Lights*], 57

Some people think that *The Zohar* is a book of ethics explaining what is appropriate behavior, and what the expected punishment should be for not behaving accordingly. Others think that *The Zohar* describes a mystical world existing somewhere out there, without any connection to man.

Another view maintains that *The Zohar* doesn't mean to tell us anything. Rather it is a book written by Kabbalists about something only they understand, and for us these matters are meaningless. They believe we only need to read *The Zohar* as a remedy for health, protection from trouble, and to bring us success in life. There are also those who think the book was not meant to be read at all, and it's enough to have it at home or at your business for the book to benefit you.

But in truth, *The Zohar* speaks only of the attributes and desires concealed within us, and of nothing else. *The Zohar* describes our "spiritual anatomy," the structure of our soul, the forces it contains, and the states it undergoes. The soul is built from spiritual organs, with names identical to those of our body's physical organs. Additionally, the soul includes everything that seems to exist in the world around us, not as material objects, but as forces and qualities. Kabbalists have said about it that man is a small world.[24]

When we open *The Zohar*, we should desire to identify all the things it mentions within us. Everything exists in the soul, and that's all *The Zohar* speaks of. The soul is the collective "will to receive" that the Creator created, and we are bound to reveal that nothing else really exists. Within that will, we want to detect all kinds of levels, qualities, and connections.

While reading, we should try to maintain that approach. When it dissipates, we should try to renew it. The truth is that we won't detect anything by ourselves, yet our effort to find the words within us enable the Light to operate upon us. Everything we read about and search for within us begins to project its "frequency" upon us. According to our passion to sense the internality of the matters, "new senses" begin to arise in us with which we can sense the true picture, the spiritual image.

> "Because Israel are destined to taste from the Tree of Life, which is this holy Book of Zohar, through it, they will be redeemed from exile."
>
> The Book of Zohar, Portion Naso, item 90

GROWING LIKE A BABY

> "The Holy Zohar connects man to infinity."
>
> Rabbi Moshe Bar-Eliyahu, The Remainder of Israel, "The Gate of Connection," Gate 1, Treatise 5, Essay 2

The Book of Zohar is the connection between us and the spiritual system. If we know how to "activate" The Zohar correctly, we receive the Light that reforms through it.

The Light operates upon us and gradually corrects us, elevates us, purifies us, builds new senses, feelings, and thoughts in us. We develop them gradually, like a baby growing from day to day.

A baby coming into the world doesn't know where it is. It just opens to perceiving the world and understanding it. Is it equipped with any instructions? It is not. It develops the senses that will reveal the world, then develops the senses further to reveal more. While reading *The Zohar*, we should work similarly. It is the most natural approach, growing like babies.

In truth, our condition is a bit more complicated. A baby is born with senses and only develops them, whereas we have no spiritual senses whatsoever. Spiritually speaking, we haven't been born. This is why *The Zohar* first builds those senses in us, meaning it gives birth to us in the spiritual sense of the word, and only then develops our new senses and raises us.

A JOURNEY INTO THE WORDS

One who has not seen the Light of The Book of Zohar has never seen Light in his life.

Rabbi Tzvi Hirsh of Ziditshov,
Ateret Tzvi [*A Crown of Glory*],
BeHaalotcha [When You Mount]

The text of *The Zohar* is built in such a way that delving into it is an adventure, like entering a dense jungle. You don't know what awaits you inside, where the trails lead, or how to come out.

At first, you don't know anything. Gradually, you begin to enter the words and see that those stories have depth. You delve in, and the text begins to affect you, and in return, you begin to work with the text. Every word and every concept become voluminous, and thus you advance.

Entering *The Zohar* is not without difficulties. The purpose of the difficulties is to shatter the corporeal intellect and emotion. It is particularly these difficulties that open our ability to comprehend and feel something new. We shatter inside and begin to feel what we are facing. The "jungle" begins to clear and we begin to feel the system in it. It is similar to monkeys jumping naturally between the trees, since it's clear to them what's going on; they and the forest are truly as one. This is also how we will become.

The Zohar has a multilevel entrance system. While traversing from level to level, you get rid of limiting ideas, perspectives, and various habits, in return for something new. You have no choice but to adapt yourself to the form until you get across. This takes place on all levels—emotional, intellectual, in comprehensions, and in perspectives. We have to go through numerous networks and sieves that continually change us into something new, until we are born.

> *"They shall shine as the brightness of the firmament ... They are the ones who exert in this brightness, called The Book of Zohar."*
>
> **The Book of Zohar,**
> **BeHaalotcha [When You Mount], item 88**

MAN IS A SMALL WORLD

> *"Man includes everything."*
>
> **Baal HaSulam, "The Meaning of Conception and Birth"**

The wisdom of Kabbalah teaches us that the world is within us. Naturally, we don't feel it. Instead, we see a wide world around us. What should we do? To help us advance toward true perception, Kabbalists wrote *The Book of Zohar* for us. *The Zohar* is a "workbook" meant to enable us to upgrade our perception of reality.

While reading *The Zohar*, we search within for everything the book describes. Moses, Aaron, David, priests, Levites, trees, animals, Creator, creature, angels, and souls are all within us. We should depict these only as our inner qualities. There is nothing besides that, no person, no world, nothing. Only my soul and the discernments within it exist, as described in *The Zohar*.

When we try to picture the names and concepts written in *The Zohar*, we're repeatedly drawn back to external, corporeal depictions. However, our attempts to depict inner qualities and desires will cause our "point in the heart" to begin to develop, and that point is the beginning of the soul.

After a period of continuous exercising, meaning reading *The Zohar*, its words will begin to arouse all kinds of sensations within us. "Moses must be this; Pharaoh is that, and here is Mount Sinai." Somehow, through the mists of disorientation, things will begin to clear up. Gradually, we'll discern different qualities and the connections among them within the soul. This is how we'll discover the entire Creation within us.

SETTING WORLDS IN MOTION

Reading *The Zohar* is akin to unintentionally pressing the buttons of a sophisticated instrument and activating a dramatic process. It's similar to a baby that's screaming and causing others to move. While it just lies there and screams, its cries affect its mother and father. The baby has no idea that factories work around the world to make its diapers, games, and all it needs to make life easy and help it to develop. This is how we affect the system of Upper Forces while reading *The Zohar*, if we want to grow.

> *"The language of The Zohar remedies the soul,*
> *even when one does not understand what it says*
> *at all. It is similar to one who enters a perfumery;*
> *even when he does not take a thing, he still*
> *absorbs the fragrance."*
>
> Rabbi Moshe Chaim Ephraim of Sudilkov,
> *Degel Machaneh Ephraim*
> [*The Banner of the Camp of Ephraim*], Excerpts

LIKE OPENING THE DOOR

If we long to open our hearts to love, *The Zohar* affects us. It is like opening the door at home for a refreshing breeze to come in from the outside.[25]

Inner Work

IT'S ALL INSIDE

The spiritual dimension has nothing to do with physical actions. It's all found in the heart. In the wisdom of Kabbalah, the heart symbolizes our desires. We should look into our hearts and make all kinds of discernments in it: how we turn it one way or another—toward ourselves, toward others, or toward the Creator. It's as if the heart has to expand in order for us to be inside it, like being in a laboratory, mixing certain substances, then directing them and observing how they work.

When using other methods, people are required to perform all sorts of actions, whereas in the wisdom of Kabbalah no external actions are required. The work is internal. This is why Kabbalah is called "the wisdom of the hidden."

RECOGNITION OF EVIL

The first phase of development, according to the wisdom of Kabbalah, is being able to recognize evil. It is written (Psalms 36:10), "In Your Light, we shall see Light." To find evil, a person first needs to draw Light through the study—a great deal of It—to discover that there is something evil within us.

Only once we discover the evil and understand what it is will it be clear to us how to transform it into good.

BEING A DROP OF SEMEN

We advance toward the unknown, spiritual dimension by drawing from it the Light that reforms. It is a force that develops our "point in the heart," the soul's "drop of semen." Our efforts elevate that drop and install it in the spiritual mechanism called "uterus." The development of the spiritual drop of semen is like the development process of the physical drop of semen, which is expanded upon in the wisdom of Kabbalah.[26]

The first stage is called "the three days of absorbing the semen." It is the first time a person feels he is connecting with the Upper One (the degree above him). Next come the "forty days of creating the offspring," and a three-month development in each of the uterus' three compartments, adding up to nine months.

By the way, time in spirituality isn't measured by the clock or any type of external, changing factors. Rather, time is the internal changes a person undergoes. The months of spiritual conception are the renewals, changes that the will to receive undergoes, which is the matter from which we are all made.

As a projection of the spiritual process, things happen in the corporeal world similarly. As it is in spirituality, in our world, blood comes from the mother to the drop of semen and develops the fetus' body. We receive a special Light from "Mother *Bina*" called *Dam* [blood], from the Hebrew word, *Domem* [still]. Why is it called still? Prior to receiving that Light, we are in a passive, still state. We don't know what to do; we only want the Upper One to influence us. We are ready for anything, as long as the Upper One bestows upon us. Then He bestows and we begin to develop as a spiritual fetus.

It's amazing to see how the processes are described in great detail in the Kabbalistic writings, spanning over hundreds of pages. They include discernments that have yet to be discovered by science, concerning research on "the stages of worldly pregnancy."

Let's return to spirituality. We'll be able to develop our initial point of desire for spirituality if we cling to the uterus wall of the Upper One like a drop of semen. When this happens, the Upper One affects us and we develop—the drop begins to grow, and special phenomena are felt in it. During the pregnancy stage, we only need to keep from disrupting the Upper One from developing us. When the stage of conception ends, we are "born," and a new kind of spiritual work begins.

> *"One who desires to exit self-love and begin the work of 'bestowal' is like one who leaves all the states in which one used to live ... entering a realm in which he has never been. Thus, he has to undergo the "conception and the impregnation-months" until he can acquire new attributes."*

Rav Baruch Shalom Ashlag (Rabash),
The Writings of Rabash, Vol. 1, "When a Woman Inseminates"

NEW CHALLENGES

It's impossible to develop without having to cope with new exercises each time, exerting ourselves to solve more complicated problems, being disappointed, falling, and rising once again. It's a bit like a child learning mathematics. People with great knowledge devise problems for him to solve, and he won't be able to advance if he doesn't try to solve them.

The entire process of growth is based on problem solving. This is how we develop in our world when on the path to spiritual development. Without having problems and obstacles provided to us on the spiritual path, we wouldn't be able to ascend to the next level.

To better understand the Creator, we must expand our tools of perception. It always feels like a void in the desire, heart, and mind at first, but then we learn how to fill it with new revelations.

> *"Every day and at each moment one should start anew, as though he had never done a thing in his life."*
>
> Baal HaSulam, Letter no. 57

THERE IS NONE ELSE BESIDES HIM

A person who advances in the spiritual process should realize that all the obstacles on the spiritual path come from the Creator. They are provided at different degrees and in all sorts of forms, according to the structure of the soul and what it needs to undergo in order to complete its spiritual correction.

We aren't meant to examine *why* we receive those specific obstacles. We'll never be able to understand the obstacles as long as we are on the degrees at which we experience them. We need to rise above them, as if not noticing them, and think only about our spiritual goal.

By overcoming the obstacles along the way to attaining the goal, we can turn them into helpers, and the goal itself is built specifically from these former obstacles.

No obstacles come to a person by chance; they are all determined according to the qualities of the soul. The way in which each soul was shattered determines the nature of the obstacles that appear in order to correct it. By yearning for the spiritual goal despite the obstacles, we correct them, and they are filled with attainment, understanding, emotion, and connection with the Creator.

> *"At the time of attainment, abundance is felt,*
> *revealed and settling precisely upon all the*
> *opposites ... and all his organs and tendons will*
> *say and testify for him that each and every one of*
> *the people in the world would cut their hands and*
> *legs seven times a day to obtain a single moment*
> *in their entire lives with such a taste as they feel."*
>
> Baal HaSulam, Letter no. 8

BY YOUR ACTIONS
WE SHALL KNOW YOU

The Creator is the force that operates in the world, "the force in the operated." He holds Creation and renews it.

He creates me, He is now building a heart and brain within me, feeling, seeing, fulfilling the senses. Now, when I see something, speak with someone, the Force that gives me a picture of reality and designs it within me—in my emotions, intellect, and everything—is called "Creator."

If He does everything, then what do I myself have to do? Only the understanding that this is the way it happens, from Him. If I want to grow, then from that tiny point of awareness, my "I" can grow. The development is in the fact that I begin to know Him in return, how He builds matter, forces, and the overall operating system.

"By Your actions shall we know You" is what the wisdom of Kabbalah says.[27] That is, when I reveal His actions in me, I attain Him, Who stands behind me and builds this entire picture in me.

> *"There is nothing more natural than to obtain*
> *contact with one's Creator, for He owns Nature.*
> *Indeed, every creature has contact with the*
> *Creator, as it is written, 'The whole earth is full*
> *of His glory,' but one neither knows nor feels it.*
> *One who is rewarded with contact with Him*

gains only the awareness, like a person who has
a treasure in the pocket but doesn't know it, and
someone comes and notifies him of what he has in
his pocket, and now he has truly become rich."

Baal HaSulam, *The Writings of the Last Generation*, Part 2

"BEHOLD, HE STANDS BEHIND OUR WALL"

People just beginning the spiritual path sometimes attain a certain revelation of spirituality through inner exertion. That revelation comes to them in an incomprehensible, obscure way, but it brings a feeling.

All of a sudden, they begin to feel that something exists, as is written, "There he stands behind our wall."[28] Something in us has changed, something has changed behind this world; something is filling it all and activating everyone.

There are situations in which that revelation is temporary and gradually dissipates, and there is an advanced state in which the revelation is received permanently. When that happens, we rise above what happened in the material world to enter the world of causes, and we feel our connection with the Creator.

And when we are rewarded with merging with the forces and the actions beyond matter, we identify with infinity.

The Internality of Torah

GO FORTH FROM YOUR COUNTRY

"Go forth from your country, from your homeland, and from your father's house, to the land that I will show you."

Genesis 12:1

Abraham is a force within us, symbolizing the beginning of the soul's development. After a man develops in life in various forms, without knowing exactly where he's going, what's going on with him and why, he begins to feel that perhaps life has a purpose he is unaware of. There is something else worth achieving in life; life is not just at the level in which we live, ending there. When a person begins to think that way, "Abraham" is said to be speaking in him.

From where did Abraham come? From "idolatry."[29] Until now, a person appreciated all types of corporeal goals, even to the point of making "idols" of them. But when one begins to ponder what one gets out of this life, eventually one breaks the idols and begins to search for something new.

Such a person searches, but doesn't know exactly what he's looking for. Then, out of that situation a person hears a voice within him saying, "You won't be able to advance as you are now. You must go to a new place, to a new outlook on life."

> *"Go forth from your country" means from your will—*
> *the desire with which one is born, namely "the desire*
> *to receive delight and pleasure," which is self-love."*
> Rav Baruch Shalom Ashlag (Rabash),
> *The Writings of Rabash*, Vol. 1, "Go Forth from Your Country"

INNER EVENTS

A person who develops spiritually finds within what is written in the holy writings. He or she experiences everything as inner events on the steps of spiritual development that "clothe" each word, each sentence, and every story in the Torah. One's inner world is built scene by scene, just as in a movie. This is how the soul develops.

"Each soul is willing to draw the souls of Moses, Aaron, Samuel, David, and Solomon within it, as times that it experiences. During the exit from Egypt and the reception of the Torah, the soul of Moses appears on it; during the seven that they conquer, the soul of Joshua; and in the building of the Temple, the soul of King Solomon."

Baal HaSulam, "600,000 Souls"

SINS AND MORE SINS

When we read the Torah, it seems like Israel constantly sin and anger the Creator. They don't listen to Him and they rebel against Him. The Creator wants to destroy them, and Moses stands between them, pleading on their behalf and protecting them. It seems as if there is no hope for the nation of Israel, and that they will always be trouble.

However, what is truly going on is the exact opposite. From the first words of the Torah, "In the beginning God created," until the last words, "In the eyes of all of Israel," the Torah speaks of one thing only: correcting the soul.

The soul consists of 613 desires[30] that we have to correct on each of the 125 spiritual degrees. We have to change how we use these desires from egoistically to altruistically, from "in order to receive" to "in order to give." The correction process takes place through the Light that reforms, which takes us from stage to stage until the end of correction. The Torah speaks only about this process, in which first an egoistic desire is revealed and then corrected. The evil is always revealed first, and only then is it corrected to good.

When what is written in the Torah is misunderstood, things definitely seem questionable. For example, as soon as the people of Israel were rewarded with exiting Egypt, they mad a golden calf. However, we should understand that this is how we advance, each time revealing evil at a higher level and correcting it. Only in this way can we move up the steps of the spiritual ladder to infinity.

"WRITE THEM DOWN ON THE SLATE OF YOUR HEART"

There is a commandment stating that each person should write a book of Torah for himself.[31] From the aspect of the internality of Torah, it means that a person should internally experience all the states written in the Torah of Moses. It speaks of spiritual degrees toward which we should rise by correcting our egoistic nature and revealing everything taking place within us.

The writing of the Torah is done on the heart, on our desires. At each degree, new desires appear in us and we must write upon them, *Taamim, Nekudot, Tagin,* and *Otiot (TANTA)*. Once we have completed writing *TANTA* on all our desires, we attain full adhesion with the Creator.[32]

> *"The purpose of creation ... [is] to elevate a person to a Higher and more important degree, to feel his God like the human sensation, which is already given to him. As one knows and feels one's friend's wishes, so will he learn the ways of the Creator, as it is written about Moses, 'And the Lord spoke unto Moses face to face, as a man speaks unto his friend.' Any person can be as Moses."*

Baal HaSulam, "The Teaching of the Kabbalah and Its Essence"

THE HOLY SCRIPTURES

> *"The internality of the wisdom of Kabbalah is none other than the internality of the Bible, the Talmud, and the legends."*

Baal HaSulam, "The Teaching of the Kabbalah and Its Essence"

The Holy Scriptures speak only of revealing the Creator to a person living in this world. The authors composing these writings were of spiritual attainment, and wrote only about revealing the spiritual life. Indeed, this is the purpose of our existence here on earth.

The scriptures merited the title "holy" because their role is to lead us to discover holiness, the quality of love and bestowal, the attribute of the Creator.

The Holy Scriptures were written in several styles. Each Kabbalist wrote according to the state of the souls in his time and according to the root of his own soul. The authors explain to us how the Creator is revealed in a person's internality in various ways, using all sorts of forms and images, directly and indirectly, obscurely and explicitly. However, we are accustomed to only seeing the superficial image of an ox that gored a cow, of David with Bat Sheba, or of nomads conquering the Land of Israel and driving out its inhabitants.

By doing so, we have lowered the holy Torah from its divine height and turned it into a historical novel, an ethics book or a constitution. We haven't connected with the author, who wanted to connect us with the Creator.

> *Woe unto one who says that the Torah comes to*
> *tell literal tales and the uneducated words of such*
> *as Esau and Laban. If this is so, even today we*
> *can turn the words of an uneducated person into*
> *law, and even nicer than theirs. And if the Torah*
> *indicates mundane matters, even the rulers of the*

world have among them better things, so let us
follow them and turn them into law in the same
way. However, all the words of the Torah have the
uppermost meaning.

The Book of Zohar with the Sulam [Ladder] Commentary,
BeHaalotecha [When You Mount], item 58

THE LANGUAGE OF THE BRANCHES

The Torah, the method of correction that Moses gave to
the nation of Israel, was written in the language of the
branches. It uses corporeal concepts (branches) to point
to spiritual elements (roots).

Kabbalists, people who attain both worlds—the
corporeal and the spiritual—can "decode" the language
of the branches. They identify which spiritual root
is specified by what corporeal branch, hence, in the
internality of Torah, they see in the Torah instructions for
inner work correcting the ego and developing the soul.

People without spiritual attainment can see only corporeal descriptions in the language of the branches. They
only see the externality of the Torah and don't think there's
anything concealed within it. This phenomenon is called
"materializing the matters,"[33] and it stems from the millennia of Israel's detachment from the spiritual world.

Until our time, Kabbalists said nothing about that. But when immigration to the Land of Israel began, indicating the end of the exile, they came out of hiding. They declared it was time to become familiar with the purpose of life through the wisdom of Kabbalah once more, something that had been forgotten since the ruin of the Temple.

The uniqueness of the wisdom of Kabbalah is that it doesn't let us treat things in a corporeal manner.[34] It describes in detail all the elements of "the will to receive" and the stages of correction of each of them, complete with sketches and calculations. Kabbalah leads us step by step up the levels of correction and teaches us what we have to do at each level and how. It doesn't let us imagine we can attain anything good in our lives unless we correct our egos, and shows us that the way to do it is through internal actions.

> "Only through the expansion of the wisdom of
> Kabbalah in the masses will we obtain complete
> redemption... Both the individual and the nation
> will not complete the aim for which they were
> created, except by attaining the internality of the
> Torah and its secrets. Therefore, we must establish
> seminaries and compose books to hasten the
> distribution of the wisdom throughout the nation."

Baal HaSulam, "Introduction to the Book, Panim Meirot uMasbirot," Item 5

The Righteous

RIGHTEOUS AND WICKED

*"It is known from books and from authors
that the Creator is benevolent. This means
that His guidance appears to the lower ones as
benevolence."*

Baal HaSulam, *Shamati*, Essay no. 34

Kabbalists write that the Creator is good and benevolent, that He created us in order to benefit us, that He loves us and cares for us. However, when we examine our lives, it seems that each of us is lacking something; we all have complaints about what is happening to us in life.

*"In that state, when they cannot say that the
Creator imparts only good, they are considered
wicked because suffering makes them condemn
their Maker. Only when they see that the Creator*

imparts them pleasure do they justify the Creator.
It is as our sages said, "Who is righteous? He who
justifies his Maker."

Baal HaSulam, *Shamati*, Essay no. 34

The wisdom of Kabbalah teaches us that to feel that the Creator is good and benevolent, we have to correct our vessels of perception. A person who does this is called a *Tzadik* [righteous/just] because only then can the Creator be justified.

This means that the Creator, the Upper Force of Nature, is good and benevolent, but we don't sense it because He created us opposite from Him, egoists. Through our correction we become similar to Him, and our vessels of perception expand.

It could be said that we are like negative charges in a large field of positive charge, and our work is to become positive and then keep growing. The degrees of drawing near the Creator, nearer to the Absolute Positive, are degrees of positivity, meaning degrees of feeling good, and they are what Kabbalah calls "degrees of righteousness."

THE FEELING IN THE HEART

"A righteous is a person immersed in the world
of the Creator... He always proceeds and receives
good and pleasant feelings, and he is immersed

in constant pleasure. Thus, he always blesses the
Creator, who created him to provide him with
such a good and joyful world."

Baal HaSulam, Letter no. 55

According to the wisdom of truth, it is impossible to feel bad and bless the Creator at the same time. Our feeling at the bottom of our hearts determines whether we are righteous or wicked, and not what we say out loud.[35]

If we feel bad in our hearts, we are surely cursing the Creator. If we feel good in our hearts, we are blessing the Creator. There is no other option. It turns out that the righteous is not one who takes misery submissively, but rather one who corrects his vessels of perception and with them can sense the true reality that is full of Light.[36]

THE THIRTY-SIX RIGHTEOUS ONES

Thirty-Six Righteous Ones[37] is a spiritual concept. It concerns a system of forces holding and maintaining reality. They are special souls through which abundance is transferred to the level of this world. The light disperses from them in various invisible ways and maintains life on different levels—still, vegetative, animate, and human. Without that light, without that energy, even the electrons wouldn't be able to move.

A Group

THEY HELPED
EVERY MAN HIS FRIEND

"One cannot raise oneself above one's circle.
Hence, one must suck from one's environment.
...If one chooses for oneself a good environment,
one saves time and efforts, since one is drawn
according to one's environment."
Baal HaSulam, *Shamati*, Essay no. 225

The people of Israel began as a group of people that Abraham gathered in ancient Babylon. They united in order to attain the spiritual world, using the method of Kabbalah that Abraham had developed. The principle of uniting into a group is the foundation of the method of Kabbalah, and why Kabbalists always bond in groups.

If we were alone in the world, we wouldn't be able to emerge from ourselves and attain spirituality. This is why the Creator divided the single soul into myriad parts. A reality was created where we live in a world with numerous people around us. From this state, if we want to attain spirituality we have to join other people who want it, too.

A particular part of the wisdom of Kabbalah explains how to behave within a group, the reciprocal spiritual work we should carry out, and how to help each other out. A single person doesn't have enough strength to emerge from himself, and needs additional strength. Within the group, he finds people who support him. They push him, he pushes them, and they all work together.

INTENTIONS LABORATORY

> "Man is created with a Kli called 'self-love'
> ...Without annulling self-love it is impossible to
> achieve Dvekut (adhesion) with the Creator,
> meaning equivalence of form. And since it is
> against our nature, we need a society that will
> form a great force so we can work together."
>
> Rabash, *The Social Writings of Rabash*, "Purpose of Society (2)"

A group is like a laboratory within which we sharpen our intentions. The laboratory includes friends, Kabbalah writings, and a Kabbalist teacher who has attained spirituality. We learn about the force of love and giving, the force of the Creator, and try to realize it in the group. We don't try it alone, in our imaginations, but with people going through the same process.

Together, we receive direction concerning what it means to increase bestowal, loving, and giving, and becoming more like the Creator. Our continuous efforts to build the quality of the Creator and develop a longing for that quality to overpower us are "the work with intentions."

A COMMON VESSEL

"Each of them had a spark of love of others, but the spark could not ignite the light of love ... so they agreed that by uniting, the sparks would become a big flame."

Rabash, *The Social Writings of Rabash*,
"One Should Always Sell the Beams of His House"

There are only two forces in reality—the force of receiving, and the force of giving, self-love and love of others. Naturally, our egos appreciate the force of receiving. The work in the group is aimed at elevating within us the importance of the force of giving.

The more we value that force, the more we appreciate it and the more we can advance. As advertisers relentlessly try to sell us useless stuff, the group should advertise the importance of the force of giving until we feel that to be loving and giving like the Creator is the greatest thing possible.

> *"There is one point we should work on—*
> *appreciation of spirituality."*

Rabash, *The Social Writings of Rabash*, "The Agenda of the Assembly"

In the group, we read together Kabbalah texts that describe our corrected state. We try to unite by rejecting the hate and disrespect we feel, and our desire to control each other. As we study, the Light that reforms gradually affects us and a common vessel forms among us. The Creator isn't revealed in me or in you, but in the bond between us. Hence, a new vessel is created in the group, within which we can feel spiritual life, the Light.

AS ONE MAN WITH ONE HEART

> *"When all human beings agree to abolish and*
> *eradicate their will to receive for themselves, and*
> *have no other desire but to bestow upon their*
> *friends, all worries and jeopardy in the world will*
> *cease to exist."*

Baal HaSulam, "Introduction to The Book of Zohar," Item 19

In our generation, all of humanity must become one large group and correct itself. To do that, Rav Baruch Shalom HaLevi Ashlag (The Rabash), Baal HaSulam's son and successor, wrote dozens of essays on the work in a group. He gave the world the doctrine of unity with a detailed guide concerning all the states existing in the relationships within the group. We study and develop spiritually according to his writings.

Technology enables us to convey the method of correction via TV and internet to anywhere in the world. Lessons on the wisdom of Kabbalah are broadcast live daily, and through them thousands of people join this group of students. Some of them gather in learning centers of "Kabbalah for All" and others join the group virtually.

Nowadays, various ways to join the group are open to anyone interested in developing spiritually. Even the physical distance between people around the world is no longer an obstacle. We are talking about creating an internal bond amongst us, and it turns out that it's possible to bond with others perfectly well through the media because it's not the bodies that connect, but the hearts.

In this large group, with branches all over the world, people differ physically, yet are very similar internally. They all want to feel they are part of one world of love, security, and prosperity, and would like to ensure better lives for their children and themselves. This is why they unite.

Eventually, the wisdom of Kabbalah should become a global method of education, offering humanity a way to be safe from harm. Kabbalah, the method of unity, will connect and unite people with a bond of mutual commitment, giving, and love.

> *"The role of the Israeli nation is to qualify the world for a certain measure of purity"*
> **Baal HaSulam, "The *Arvut* [Mutual Guarantee]," Item 21**

Kabbalah and Religion

MITZVOT [COMMANDMENTS]– CORRECTIONS OF THE DESIRE

Question: What is the significance of *Mitzvot* [Commandments] on the spiritual path?

In spirituality, performing the *Mitzvot* has a different meaning than what we're accustomed to—*Mitzvot* are corrections of the desire. The wisdom of Kabbalah explains that the soul consists of 613 desires.[38] We have to correct our use of them from egoistic to altruistic, from "in order to receive" to "in order to bestow."

Each such correction is called "performing a *Mitzva* [singular for *Mitzvot*]," and the sum of all the corrections of the desire is called "performing 613 *Mitzvot*."[39]

How do we correct the egoistic desires? We correct them with the Light that reforms, which comes with the study of Kabbalah. This is how we gradually attain equivalence with the Creator and the revelation of the spiritual world.

Because *Mitzvot* are performed in spirituality, Kabbalists set up customs in the corporeal world—*Tefillin*, *Talit*, *Mikveh* [ritual bathing], *Kashrut* [Kosher food], and so on.

Where did these customs come from? How do we know how to perform them? Ever since Abraham gathered a group of Kabbalists around him, who over the years became the nation of Israel, that nation felt the spiritual world. It lived with a clear sense of the comprehensive force of nature, the force of love and bestowal. The same people who attained spirituality felt the Upper Roots and pointed to their branches in this world. They tell us how the Upper Forces are emulated in the material world, and accordingly define which customs to carry out and how.

The spiritual world and the corporeal world were one reality to them, an entire complex. They performed the *Mitzvot* in spirituality, and the customs in corporeality. However, after the ruin of the Temple, spirituality disappeared and the people were left with only corporeal customs. As a result, they began to treat the customs as *Mitzvot*, whereas the internal, spiritual existence, the correction of the desire, was forgotten.[40]

> *"The Torah and the Mitzvot were given only to purify Israel, to develop in us the sense of recognition of evil, imprinted in us at birth. This is generally defined as our self-love, and to come to the pure good defined as the 'love of others,' which is the one and only passage to the love of the Creator."*
>
> Baal HaSulam, "The Freedom"

WHAT'S IMPORTANT TO THE CREATOR?

It is written in *Midrash Rabah*: "The *Mitzvot* [commandments] were given only to purify people with them. Why would He, the Creator, care who butchers from the throat and who butchers from the back of the neck?"[41] In other words, the Creator doesn't care how we butcher beasts, whether at the throat or at the back of the neck, meaning in a Kosher way or not. What *is* important to Him is the purification and cleansing of people.

We'll explain the above. As we said, there are 613 desires in our will to receive, all of which are directed toward ourselves. Using the desires in that way is considered a transgression. Correcting the desires to the benefit of others is called a *Mitzva* [commandment/ good deed] Reversing the direction of the desire's action from inward to outward is called "repentance."[42] This is all we need to do in this world, because the substance from which we are made is no more than desire, as Baal HaSulam explains in the "Preface to the Wisdom of Kabbalah."

This is why the Creator doesn't care how we butcher beasts and the like, but cares what we do with our hearts, with our desires.[43] Correcting the desire from "in order to receive" to "in order to bestow" is also called "correcting the soul," and it is what brings us to equivalence with the Creator. This is the whole story in a nutshell; nothing else exists in this reality.

Having said that, a question still arises, "What about all the customs of Israel we have been familiar with for generations?" Indeed, these are the culture of the Israeli nation, a framework of existence meant to preserve us as the nation of Israel. We should respect that framework, as it has maintained us for thousands of years, but it has no effect on the soul's correction. Eventually, all the nations will have to correct their souls, and they'll do that without keeping kosher and the like.

To summarize, there is a fundamental difference between correcting the soul, and honoring the nation of Israel's traditional framework of existence. Today, we are obligated to recognize that difference and put everything in its place.[44]

THE RELIGION OF LOVE

"The purpose of creation applies to the entire human race, none absent."

Baal HaSulam, "The Love of the Creator and Love of Man"

In the future society, all people will aspire to live according to the principle, "Love your neighbor as yourself." Members of all religions and people of all nations will live according to a single comprehensive "religion," in which there will be only one principle—the love of others as a means of revealing the Creator.

In Baal HaSulam's *The Writings of the Last Generation*, that religion is called "a common religion for all the nations," "an equal religion for the entire world," "the religion of love of others," "a religion of altruism," and "a religion of love." By "religion," Baal HaSulam means the method of correcting human nature as suggested by Kabbalah. This can also be seen in his essay, "The Essence of Religion and Its Purpose." Baal HaSulam emphasizes "The religious form of all nations, 'Love your neighbor as yourself'... But otherwise, each nation may pursue its own religion and traditions, and one must not interfere with the other."[45]

Kabbalah is the universal method of correction. It respects religion as a traditional, cultural framework for each nation. But beyond culture, everyone—Jews, Christians, Muslims, members of all religions and all nations—will have to correct their souls through the method of Kabbalah.

Clashes between religions, which have taken place throughout history, stem from the fact that each religion claims ownership of the Creator, the next world, and the definition of reward and punishment. But as soon as we understand that no religion has any contact with the spiritual level of existence, or with the correction of the soul, the dividing factor is neutralized in all religions, and the disrespect and hatred of others disappear. Each nation may remain with its traditional customs, and the differences between nations and cultures actually create the rich, human texture.

THE CREATION OF THE WORLD

Question: How does Kabbalah relate to the contradiction between the creation of the world 5,773 years ago and the Big Bang theory?

The Big Bang took place approximately 14 billion years ago. Its cause was a spark of the Upper Light that reached its lowest degree, enveloped in egoism. The spark included all the matter and energy of our world, and from it the entire universe later developed.

Planet Earth formed approximately 4.6 billion years ago, as part of our solar system. For several billion years Earth's crust cooled down until the atmosphere and life came into being.[46]

Nothing is coincidental. The entire development was a manifestation of the information found in that initial spark.

After the inanimate nature, vegetative, animate, and human nature appeared. The interpretation of evolution based on the external form we observe—meaning the appearance of a species developing from a previous species, from which another species developed—isn't true. The reason each element in Nature appears is the information rooted from the start in the spark of light. Evolution is actually a process of revealing (developing) data pieces (genes), which Kabbalah calls *Reshimot* [recollections].

Hundreds of thousands of years ago, man developed from the ape, as the ARI also writes in *Tree of Life*,"[47] but only 5,773 years ago (true to the date of writing those lines), a desire to reveal the Creator first arose in a human being. The day he began to reveal the Creator is considered "the day of Creation," spiritually speaking, since this is when the spiritual development of the human race began. However, it doesn't refer to the time of the material creation of the world, which took place billions of years previously.

THE WISDOM OF THE HIDDEN

We study our world through science to reveal what has been concealed from us. However, there is another part to reality, a concealed world, a higher world, which science cannot reveal. To sense that part of reality, one has to correct one's nature, the ego. Only then can one begin to sense the concealed world and study it in a scientific manner.

All the different faiths and religions are theories of the concealed world (of God), and of things that this world commits us to do. These theories vary and even contradict one another. They all exist because that part of reality is concealed from us. None of them provides a practical method of revealing the concealed world (revealing God).

Kabbalists are people who acquired the qualities of love and giving, through which they attained the concealed world. They describe the structure of the Upper World and offer the option of revealing it to all who want it. They do not require us to change our way of life, since there is no connection between corporeal actions and the acquisition of the quality of love and giving. Here, it isn't about having faith in God, but about revealing the Creator.

Kabbalah and Science

KABBALAH–THE ROOT OF ALL SCIENCES

"This wisdom is no more and no less than a sequence
of roots, which hang down by way of cause and
consequence, by fixed, determined rules, interweaving
to a single, exalted goal described as the revelation of
His Godliness to His creatures in this world."

Baal HaSulam,
"The Essence of the Wisdom of Kabbalah"

The wisdom of Kabbalah is actually the root of all sciences, since it speaks of the collective force of all reality–the Creator. This force surrounds the entire reality and includes our world and the Upper Worlds. The whole of reality is included in this single force.

Kabbalah explains to us how it works, what its purpose is, how it governs us, and what it wants from us. When we reveal the collective force and all its parts, which fill the entire reality, we also understand the purpose of each part's existence in reality and how best to use it.

> *"The greatest wonder about this wisdom is the integration in it. That is, all the elements of the vast reality proceed by it, integrate, intertwine, and unite until they come into a single thing—the Almighty—who includes them together."*
>
> Baal HaSulam,
> "The Teaching of the Kabbalah and Its Essence"

THE REVEALED AND THE CONCEALED

The world is revealed to us through our five senses. The sum of what we receive by researching our surroundings constitutes our science. It was only out of convenience that we divided it into separate fields such as physics, chemistry, and biology, and there are many phenomena that we still don't sense, so no science yet exists in their regard. We might discover these areas tomorrow and begin to study them, thus expanding our science.

However, there are phenomena in reality that are not within the range of our senses. We won't be able to perceive spiritual phenomena, even if we develop superb technology and incredible instruments to enhance our senses because our senses operate through absorption, whereas spirituality can be revealed only through bestowal and giving, when we emerge from ourselves outward, to others. This part of reality, which will always remain concealed from our egoistic perception, is called the Upper World, the spiritual world.

So how do we advance? The Upper Force of Nature, which created us as egoistic beings, can also change us if we know how to draw it near to us. When the Upper World is revealed to us, we will begin to study it and document its phenomena. This is how the Upper Science is created, and how the wisdom of Kabbalah developed.

EXTERNAL WISDOMS

"To move a step forward in a scientific manner, all we need is the wisdom of Kabbalah, for all the teachings in the world are included in the wisdom of Kabbalah."

Baal HaSulam, "The Freedom"

The wisdom of Kabbalah explains reality to us, starting from the initial point from which it was created. It describes how this reality descends and cascades through all the Upper Worlds down to our world. Our world is the last degree of this descent, and emulates all the details existing in the spiritual degree above it.

Kabbalists refer to the wisdom of this world as "external wisdoms" because all the wisdoms and sciences we have in this world lack internality—the understanding of where things stem from and why. They lack recognition of the Emanator, the Upper Force governing everything through cause and effect.

OBSERVING FROM ABOVE

When a scientist studies Nature, he or she takes a certain substance, manipulates it in some way, such as heating it or cooling it, and measures the substance's reaction to the manipulations. A scientist seemingly observes from above. We can perform such actions regarding the lower degrees in Nature—inanimate, vegetative, and animate, but we can't do it on ourselves.

We cannot truly rise above ourselves and study ourselves from above. To learn what humans are, we must observe them from the degree above the human level. This is why psychology and psychiatry, which study the "human" problems of people—their desires and thoughts—are not the same type of science as the natural sciences. However we may advance in those fields, matters will remain unclear. We may learn a little more, but we won't be able to truly permeate the depths of the human heart and the mind. Understanding those depths is impossible without the inner wisdom, the wisdom of Kabbalah.

Kabbalah deals with the internality of human beings, observing the substance we are made of and revealing how we are governed, respond, and operate. Kabbalah enables us to ascend to the level from which we are governed and study ourselves from there.

> "Just as a person should adapt to the material nature and its forces, just so and even more should one adapt to the rules of the spiritual nature, which have more dominance over the entire reality ... and are more dominant in the whole of one's interior."
>
> The Raiah Kook,
> *Orot HaKodesh* [*Lights of Sanctity*] 4, p 440

A SPIRITUAL MICROSCOPE

In all of Creation, only two forces exist, two qualities: The Light (quality of bestowal), and the desire for pleasure (quality of reception), which the Light created.

Everything else stems from them. It is similar to mathematics, in which there is zero and something else, and the whole of mathematics stems from those two.

The wisdom of Kabbalah allows us to develop an "inner microscope" through which we can "see" spiritual forces, forces of bestowal. "Seeing" means feeling and understanding them. However, to measure and become familiar with those forces, we need to have bestowing forces ourselves.

After acquiring the force of bestowal, we develop it like a super sensitive microscope that we can focus in different ways, permeating the depth of the substance (desire), and observing the different phenomena within it (receiving-bestowing) according to the sensitivity of our vessels of perception.

> *"It is an unbending rule for all Kabbalists that 'anything we do not attain, we do not define by a name and a word.'"*
>
> Baal HaSulam,
> "The Essence of the Wisdom of Kabbalah"

WHAT NEXT?

Science cannot elevate us to a higher degree of existence because we can't change our nature by it. Science only comes to help us fulfill our desires.

Let's illustrate that. Suppose we could completely satisfy ourselves and be as satisfied as possible at all times: eating endlessly, hearing endlessly, seeing endlessly—everything to the fullest and ceaselessly. Then what? Science can't take us to another level of existence.

The wisdom of Kabbalah, on the other hand, builds in us a new nature. It elevates us to the degree of the Upper Force and provides us with new desires and infinite fulfillments.

It turns out that there is a fundamental difference between science and Kabbalah. Science provides us with knowledge that can help us improve our condition in this world, whereas Kabbalah elevates us to the Upper World. Hence, in our generation, when this world isn't enough for us, the wisdom of Kabbalah is being revealed.

> *"Where the wisdom of researches ends, the wisdom of Kabbalah begins."*
> Rabbi Nachman of Breslev, *Talks of the Moharan*, p 225

Spirituality

THE PURPOSE OF EXISTENCE

Question: What is really the purpose of our existence?

The purpose of our existence is to reach infinity, meaning a boundless existence in time, place, motion, perception, and fulfillment. This is spiritual life—living in harmony, unity, understanding, and attainment. All our desires manifest in full and we can do *anything*. It is the degree in which the created being equalizes with the Creator.

WITHIN US

"Spirituality is the source of life and pleasure."

Baal HaSulam,
Shamati, Essay no. 145

The loose end to spirituality is within us, much deeper than all our present desires. Beyond our desires for food, sex, family, money, honor, power, and knowledge, there is a private, important, and great desire, a spiritual one. When the spiritual desire, namely "the point in the heart," awakens in us we are drawn to reveal the meaning of life. That point is the beginning of the eternal piece within us. The more we become familiar with the point and expand it, the more we'll identify with it and see the life therein.

These are very high sensations, internal and exciting. We begin to realize that the material life was only given to us so we could develop the spiritual life within that point. As the point grows, we reveal an entire reality within it, a world, an internal dimension we hadn't felt before.

> *"That worm, born inside a radish, lives there and thinks that the world is like the radish it was born in. But as soon as it breaks the shell of the radish and peeps out, it claims in bewilderment: 'I thought the whole world was the size of the radish I was born in. Now I see a grand, beautiful, and wondrous world before me!'"*

Baal HaSulam,
"Introduction to the Book of the Zohar," Item 40

THERE IS LIFE AFTER MIDDLE AGE

*"But when half his life is through, begin the days
of the decline, which, by their content, are his
dying days. This is because a person does not die
in an instant, just as he did not receive his life
in an instant. Rather his candle, being his ego,
withers and dies bit by bit."*

Baal HaSulam, "The Freedom"

At middle age, many people begin to decline. They are accustomed to this life and know they won't achieve more than they have. This is when they begin to decline. Their desires and passions burn out until they eventually find no further purpose in life.

But when one attains spiritual life, things will work the other way around. A person constantly attains more. The desires undergo incessant upgrading, and one constantly moves like a pendulum—from right to left to right—building oneself in the "middle line." Such a person continues to realize oneself and develop spiritually through one's last moment in our world, since spiritual growth never ends.

SPIRITUALITY = BESTOWAL

Spirituality is bestowal, love, and pure giving. It is the ability to act without demanding any reward for yourself—not in money, honor, good feeling, or drawing blessing to yourself or to your relatives and so on.

Spirituality is the opposite of the corporeal nature, which is based entirely on reception for ourselves. Our nature doesn't allow us to do anything unless we gain something by it.[48] One way or another, we don't make a move unless it serves our interests. That's our nature. Spirituality, however, exists above it, opposite from it.

WHERE IS SPIRITUALITY?

Spirituality is not "there"; it's here, between us, within us. If we want to feel spirituality, we need to acquire a spiritual quality, a quality of bestowal and love. When we have that quality, we are near spirituality, and when we don't—we are far from it.

NO COERCION IN SPIRITUALITY

Question: Does implementing the spiritual process on a daily basis in relationships with kin, coworkers, or friends mean working on our attributes, like anger and the like?

We will never be able to truly change our attributes. However, as a result of the blows we suffer from society, and because of being shamed and degraded, we learn to hide the things that pained us. We do not change the qualities themselves, but create an external "face" toward society.

The wisdom of Kabbalah doesn't go against human nature or attempt to break it. It simply says, "Forget about the attributes with which you were born and lived up to now; don't bother with them. Leave them be. Don't force yourself, there is no coercion in spirituality."[49] As you proceed along your way you will see how those attributes assist your development without artificially "bending" them. In the meantime you should build another part within you, regardless of what is in you now.

It is not easy to perceive this point. Indeed, everyone talks about needing to be better people, but they mean correcting the attributes with which they were born. Kabbalah, on the other hand, doesn't deal with that at all. Even when Kabbalists talk about "Love your neighbor as yourself," they don't mean what we mean when we think of "love" of others. They're referring to a completely new approach to reality.

In other words, the wisdom of Kabbalah doesn't tell a person, "You must love others." Rather, it builds a seemingly new sense within, with which one begins to sense the concealed part of reality. Gradually, an image appears in which we are all connected as parts of a single body, and the love of others inevitably bursts out.

> *"One can coerce and enslave oneself to anything,*
> *but no coercion or enslavement in the world will*
> *help with love."*
>
> Baal HaSulam,
> "Introduction to the Study of the Ten Sephirot," Item 66

CONNECTING THE SPARKS

As scientists research our world, Kabbalists research the Upper World and reveal it. In their words, "a spiritual world" means that we are all connected with each other, not in our bodies but internally.

From that inner part that connects us in the spiritual world, there is now a tiny spark within us, a spark desiring something higher than this world, drawing us back to spirituality. That spark exists deep within us and is called "the point in the heart."

For now the spark is wrapped in an egoistic heart, which is why we don't feel it wants to unite with others. However, if we correct the ego within us and begin to feel the spiritual world, we will discover that ascending the spiritual degrees also means ascending in the inner bond between us. That bond creates a common vessel within which a great Light is felt ever stronger.

Intellect and Emotion

THE HEART KNOWS

"The will in any essence creates needs, and the needs create thoughts and concepts so as to obtain those needs, which the will to receive demands."

Baal HaSulam,
"Introduction to The Book of Zohar," Item 21

We are emotional beings. When a certain desire arises in us, we feel the need for something and the intellect goes into action. It helps us understand what we want to feel and how we can obtain what we desire. Mistakenly, people measure themselves and those around them by their intellects, but the truth is that the intellect is a servant to the desire. After all, the substance that was created is desire.

In spiritual development, the corporeal intellect determines nothing. The understanding goes through the heart, through changing the desire. It is an emotional development wherein we acquire desires of a new quality. These desires spur a new intellect in us, a spiritual one, which helps us continue to climb the 125 degrees of spiritual attainment.

THE GOLDEN MEAN

"A person cannot sustain one's body in the world without having some knowledge of the orders of corporeal nature, such as knowing which toxins are lethal, and which things burn and cause harm. Precisely so, one's soul has no right to exist ... unless it has acquired some knowledge of the orders of the nature of the systems of the spiritual worlds, the changes therein, their couplings, and what they beget."

Baal HaSulam,
"From within My Flesh Shall I See God"

The wisdom of Kabbalah is a unique wisdom. On the one hand, it discusses emotions such as hatred and love. On the other hand, its language is scientific, using concepts of worlds and *Sephirot*, vessels and lights, sketches and tables.

The emotional vs. the technical-scientific languages seem to be somewhat distant from each other, but in order to develop emotionally and attain our spiritual goal, we need examinations and measurements. We observe the desire, measuring the qualities of the soul developing in us in relation to the qualities of the Creator. The intellect helps us direct, align, grade, divide, and weigh the emotions.

In our world, too, we can't develop without integrating intellect and emotion. If an individual has only intellect without emotion, he or she is like a machine, and if one is all emotion and no intellect, he or she is incapable of reason. The wisdom of Kabbalah teaches us to find the golden mean between emotion and intellect, so that a person is filled with the correct filling, one that truly pays off.

HIGHER THRILLS

"The more one is developed, the more one senses."

Baal HaSulam,
"The General Quality of the Wisdom in of the Hidden"

By the nature of our creation, we aspire to enjoy life, to feel good. The intellect analyzes the data it receives and leads us to what it thinks will yield the greatest pleasure.

It shows us how to invest minimum energy to achieve maximum pleasure at every given moment. This process is the basis for each of our thoughts and actions, and the intellect develops through it.

Throughout the whole of human history, we have absorbed impressions from different forms of existence. Without them, our intellect and emotions would not develop. It is no coincidence, for example, that the Industrial Revolution led people out of their villages to the city. That process took place because we had to mingle with each other, develop technology, science, society, and culture to advance from the primitive life.

According to the data and impressions we accumulate at every stage, we build different social systems, which we then change. Socialism, communism, capitalism, dictatorship, democracy, religion, science, technology, various forms of education, social, and cultural revolutions—we tried all of these, only to finally realize that we had no idea how to keep content for long.

Now, having tried everything, we realize that everything we have achieved isn't enough. This is the root of the collective crisis we are experiencing in all areas of life. The sense of being at a "dead end" arises in our hearts and minds when we anticipate greater thrills than we receive in our present life. We are searching all around us, but to no avail. It is a sign that we are ready to rise from the corporeal dimension and develop spiritually.

In summary, all of humanity is now like a villager a moment before arriving at the city. At this point, the wisdom of Kabbalah is being revealed, as if saying, "Would you like something new? Be my guest!"

Prayer

WORKING ON MY SELF

*"Prayer is work in the heart. It means that since
a person's heart is the will to receive by its root,
and one needs to invert it to be only to bestow
and not to receive, it follows that one has much
work inverting it."*

Rabash, *The Writings of Rabash*, Vol. 1,
"Three Times in the Work"

The spiritual correction takes place through inner
work called "prayer." Praying means clarifying with
myself who I am, what I am, and what I want.

TO WHOM DO I PRAY?

Question: If "Man is a small world," as written
in *The Zohar*, and everything is within me,
then to whom should I actually direct my prayer?

We turn inward, toward ourselves, because the whole of reality is within us.

Where is God and who is He? God is a concept referring to a spiritual quality existing deep inside us called "*Zeir Anpin*." Currently, it is hidden from us and we have to reveal it. The term, *Boreh* [Creator], also directs us inward—*Bo* [come] *Re'eh* [see], meaning rise above your ego and you will see the Creator within you.

There are numerous levels within us. Each time we seek change, we turn to a higher level, which is still concealed, and demand assistance for the lower level. It is called "turning upward and receiving help." We turn to the higher degree within us, which we would like to attain, and from which we want to receive the correcting force. Resembling the Creator happens within us, in our corrected qualities. This is what the wisdom of Kabbalah teaches—that the Creator is revealed in "the Inner Light" within us.

We will proceed in the right direction to unify with the Creator only with this approach to the perception of reality—that the Creator exists within, but is concealed, and we desire to "penetrate" Him and hold onto Him with our internality.

AN IMPASSABLE LAW

If we imagine and pray to someone out there in the heavens to benefit us, we won't be able to correct our qualities. We have to pray to what exists within, to our more advanced state, called our "Upper One." We say, "My more corrected state, I want to connect with you; you are God to me."

What is "you?" It is I, when I am more loving, giving, and more connected with others.

It is similar to a child who wants to be a pilot. He imagines himself in the cockpit, flying his plane over his mother's house and waving to her. He imagines himself, not anyone else, in a more advanced state. This is how we should think of attaining our more advanced degree, and then aspire to it.

If we think that way, we won't make mistakes. If we think otherwise, we'll be praying to the wall. For thousands of years, humanity has been crying to the heavens in vain. We expect the Creator to pity us, and nothing happens. The situation is growing worse and more threatening each day.

It is time for us to wake up and realize that nothing good will happen until we change ourselves. Everything depends only on correcting human nature according to the Upper Nature, the nature of love and giving.

FROM THE BOTTOM OF THE HEART

In the times of the second Temple, the members of the great assembly established the institutionalized prayers. They had attained sublime spirituality and knew that the nation was about to enter a state of exile, detachment from the feeling of the spiritual world. Therefore, they prepared a sort of adaptor whose role was to maintain a certain indirect connection between the nation and spirituality. The prayers depict the corrected state that the composers of the prayers had attained. The prayers were written as examples of what we will achieve by correcting the egoism in us.

There is a fundamental difference between reading the eloquent words of the prayers out of a prayer book, and attaining the spiritual state in which we experience them. In spirituality, the prayers are built in our desires, letter by letter, word by word, sentence by sentence, by joining "vessels and Lights." This joining creates *TANTA* (*Taamim*, *Nekudot*, *Tagin*, *Otiot* [trans. Flavors, dots, tags, letters]), which combine into words and sentences. Hence, a genuine prayer is built from within.

Pleasure

A TINY CANDLE

If we combined all the pleasures humans have felt since the dawn of humanity until now, they would be only a "tiny candle" compared to the pleasure experienced in the spiritual world.

It is such an intense pleasure that we couldn't contain it in our present vessels. Hence, climbing the spiritual world requires upgrading our vessels.[50]

THE MOMENT AFTER THE ENCOUNTER

"The Light of pleasure is the progenitor of life."
Baal HaSulam, "Introduction to the book,
Panim Meirot uMasbirot," Item 19

The wisdom of Kabbalah teaches us that our sense of life is based on the moments of encounter of pleasure and desire, the moments when our desires are filled. This is why we constantly search for whatever other delights we can find. Gum, candy, ice-cream, internet, movies, traveling, vacation, anything...

The media and the people around us also provide additional options for pleasure. Yet, when we realize that, despite all the means we have, our hearts are still empty, it's a sign we are ready to develop further.

"The whole problem is that pleasure is short-lived and the suffering is long-lived."

Baal HaSulam, *The Writings of the Last Generation*, Chapter 2, "The Direction of Life"

ENJOYING WISELY

"The will to receive is the whole substance of Creation from beginning to end. Thus, all the creatures, all their innumerable instances and conducts that have appeared and that will appear, are but measures and various denominations of the will to receive. All that exists in those creatures, that is, all that is received in the will to receive imprinted in them, extends from His Essence existence from existence. It is not at all a new creation, since

it is not new at all. Rather, it extends from His
Endlessness existence from existence."

Baal HaSulam,
"Preface to the Wisdom of Kabbalah," Item 1

The fundamental matter of Creation is "the will to receive delight and pleasure," the desire to enjoy. We can't rid ourselves of that matter, since it is the basis of life.

The intensity of the desire is the discerning factor between the still, vegetative, animate, and human. A rock aspires to remain a rock, to maintain its existence. A plant wants to move toward the sun and send roots into the ground. An animal wants more. It moves about freely and bears offspring. The most developed degree is the desire that exists in humans.

We desire to derive the greatest pleasure, which causes us to want to enjoy everything good that the world can offer. However, we also find pleasure in others' misfortune. That type of desire doesn't exist in any of the other degrees in Nature. It stems from us being social creatures that feel others and compare ourselves to them. As a result, people try to acquire as much as possible, finding pleasure at the expense of others, which leads us to clash with each other.[51]

The wisdom of Kabbalah teaches us how to enjoy wisely, how to rise above the individual desire for pleasure and build a desire for collective pleasure. In such a united desire, we will discover that it is possible to enjoy limitlessly. Each one of us will begin to enjoy being free and not having to struggle for everything at every moment. We will all support each other and achieve true peace and delight.

We will suddenly feel we can enjoy everything everyone has. Until now we have been trying to draw as much as possible for ourselves, and when we found something to enjoy, that enjoyment was brief and quickly dissipated. Everything was uncertain and fragile. But now we can enjoy what there is all over the world. We aren't limited any more; the others aren't limited, and we all enjoy the peacefulness, tranquility, love, and bestowal that reside among everyone.

It turns out that the substance from which we are made, the desire for pleasure, hasn't changed, but that the way we use it has been upgraded.

> *"What is the evil in us, for which we have no*
> *delight and pleasure? It is no less and no more*
> *that the self-love within us that is keeping us from*
> *receiving the delight and pleasure."*
>
> Rabash, *The Writings of Rabash*, Vol. 1,
> "A Righteous Who Is Content; a Righteous Who Is Discontent"

A FLOW OF PLEASURE

The method that Kabbalah suggests to satisfy our desire for pleasure is based on a flow of pleasure. The problem in our current situation is that we constrain the pleasure within us, hence the sensation of pleasure ceases. However, if the pleasure could pass through us to others, a limitless flow would be created, a flow that would not stop anywhere. In this way, we would not feel life as states of filling with pleasure and states of ceasing to sense it, but as eternal pleasure.

CONSTANT PLEASURE

"One should exert with all his strength to arrive at such a permanent degree in which one will proceed and receive constant abundance and every pleasantness in constant pleasure ... pleasantness upon pleasantness."

Baal HaSulam, Letter no. 55

At the end of the day, any pleasure that ends is worthless. It doesn't matter how long that pleasure lasted—a moment, an hour, a day or even a year—if it eventually disappears, it isn't worth much.

In spirituality, the pleasure is eternal and cumulative. I derive pleasure now, later, and ever more.

Afterword

"Abundance itself resembles the vast ocean.
Some draw with a thimble;
others draw with a pail."

Rabash, *The Writings of Rabash*, Vol. 1,
"The Merit of the Small One"

"The point in the heart" can no longer proceed with the dull routine of life. It can still be confused here and there, but it won't last long. It already wants more and is not willing to compromise. It needs Light, love, and true joy. It certainly deserves to receive the best there is. This is why it has led you to this encounter with the wisdom of Kabbalah.

May your path onward be successful!

The Editors

Notes

1   Babylonian Talmud, 52a

2   Ecclesiastes 2:13

3   For more on that see Baal HaSulam's essay, "The Peace."

4   "The Creator is all bestowal, and has nothing of the form of reception, for He lacks nothing and needs to receive nothing from the creatures He has created." (Baal HaSulam, the essay "Peace in the World.")

5   Isaiah, 14:14

6   "For six thousand years there is the world," *Babylonian Talmud*, Sanhedrin 97a

7   Kabbalah books depict two ways by which the world can come to the required correction: "the path of suffering" and "the path of awareness." For more on this matter, see Baal HaSulam's *The Writings of The Last Generation*, beginning of Part One; and in *Kabbalah for the Student*, essays "Introduction to the Book, *Panim Meirot uMasbirot*," Item 7; "Introduction to the Book of Zohar," Item 16; "The Mind's Control over the Body" in "The Freedom."

8   "And in that, we are like a pile of nuts united into one body from the outside by a sack wrapping and assembling them. The extent of that unity doesn't turn them into a unified body, and the slightest movement made upon the sack, results in their running around and separating from each other. As a

result, they form partial unifications and combinations that are constantly renewed. And the whole deficiency is that they lack the natural unity from within, and their strength to bond stems from external instances. ...this pains the heart gravely ... and the only hope is to arrange for ourselves fundamental reeducation, disclosing and rekindling the dimmed out love within us." Baal HaSulam, "The Individual and the Nation."

9 "I am the Lord, I have called You in righteousness, I will also hold You by the hand and watch over You, and I will appoint You as a covenant to the people, as a light to the nations" (Isaiah, 42:6).

10 Had Israel guarded good deeds ... the... nations would not have dominated them. However, Israel are causing the rest of the nations to raise their heads in the world" *The Book of Zohar*, Portion *VaYechi* [And Jacob Lived, item 412.

11 Baal HaSulam, "Introduction to The Book of Zohar," Item 70

12 Baal HaSulam, "Introduction to the Book of Zohar," Item 71

13 "The point in the heart should be a place of sanctity in which the Light of the Creator dwells, as is written 'And I dwelled within them.' Therefore, one should try to build one's building of holiness, and the building should be fit for the Upper abundance to enter it, called 'abundance bestowed from the Giver to the receiver.' But there must be equivalence of form between the Giver and the receiver, as it is known that the receiver also has to have the intention to bestow like the Giver. This is called 'Making,' as is written 'And they shall make Me a temple.'" Rav Baruch Shalom Ashlag (Rabash), *The Writings of Rabash*, Vol. 3, "The Point in the Heart"

14 See Rabbi Baruch Shalom Ashlag, Essays "Steps of the Ladder," The Importance of the Prayer of Many."

15 "All the innovations begin only after one is rewarded with emerging from self-reception. This is the meaning of the prohibition to teach idol worshippers Torah, since when one is in Egypt, he cannot be a Jew, as he is enslaved to Pharaoh King of Egypt. ...Only after one exits Egypt, meaning self-reception,

he can be a servant of the Creator, and then he can be rewarded with Torah." Rav Baruch Shalom Ashlag (Rabash), *The Writings of Rabash*, Vol. 3, "The First Innovation"

16 "We call the elements of the reality of the Upper Worlds 'Lights,' as they bring those who attain them abundance of light and pleasure." Baal HaSulam, "The Teaching of Kabbalah and its Essence."

17 Babylonian Talmud, *Kidushin*, 30b

18 "Alone, it is impossible that one will be able to go against nature, since the matter of mind and heart, in which one must be complemented, necessitates receiving assistance, and that assistance is through the Torah, as our sages said, 'I have created the evil inclination, I have created the Torah as a spice.' This is so because while engaging in it, the Light in it reforms them" (Rabash, *The Writings of Rabash*, Vol. 1, "What Is Torah and Work on the Path of the Creator"). "Torah refers to the Light clothed in the Torah" (Baal HaSulam, *Shamati*, Essay no. 6.) "The Torah is Simple Light that expands from His Essence, whose sublimity is endless." Baal HaSulam, "Introduction to the book, From the Mouth of a Sage." See also *Midrash Raba*, *Eicha*, Introduction, Paragraph no. 2.

19 *Babylonian Talmud, Kidushin* 70a

20 Attributed to Baal Shem Tov, in the book *Maor Eynayim* [Light of the Eyes], Portion *Hukat*.

21 "It is written, 'The whole earth is full of His glory,' as it is written in The Holy *Zohar*, 'There is no place vacant of Him.' We don't feel it is because we lack the vessel for sensing, just as we see that the radio receives all the sounds existing in the world, since the receiving apparatus doesn't make the sounds, rather the sounds exist in the reality of the world. Prior to having the receiving apparatus, we wouldn't sense the sounds although they existed in reality. Likewise, we can understand that 'There is no place vacant of Him,' but we need the receiving apparatus. The receiving apparatus is called *Dvekut* [adhesion] and 'equivalence of form,' being the will to bestow. And when we have that machine, we will immediately feel that there is no place vacant of Him, but that 'The whole earth is full of His glory.'" Rabash, *The Writings of Rabash*, Vol. 3, "By Your Actions We Know You

22 For more on that, see Baal HaSulam's essay, "The Essence of the Wisdom of Kabbalah."

23 *The Book of Zohar* with the *Sulam* commentary, "The Donkey Driver."

24 *The Book of Zohar* with the *Sulam* [Ladder] Commentary, Portion *Lech Lecha* [Go Forth], item 330; and Portion Pinhas, item 859.

25 For more on the topic of *The Book of Zohar* and the correct approach to its study, see Dr. Michael Laitman's, *Unlocking the Zohar*.

26 See Baal HaSulam's *The Study of the Ten Sephirot* on the main principles of the Kabbalah of the ARI, Parts 10-12

27 For more, see Rabash, *The Writings of Rabash*, Vol. 3, "By Your Actions We Know You"

28 Song of Songs 2:9

29 "And his father and mother and the entire nation are idol worshippers, and he [Abraham] worshipped with them. And his heart wanders and understands, until he attained the path of truth, and understood the line of justice through his correct mind ... And he broke the images and began to notify the nation that there is no worthy worship other than of the God of the world" (Maimonides, *Mishneh Torah, Book of Science*, "Laws of Idolatry," 10-12).

30 "As the body has 248 organs and 365 tendons, the soul, too, has 613, which are the channels of the soul by which the bounty extends. And these channels are opened through the Torah" (Baal HaSulam, *Shamati*, Essay no. 162).

31   Maimonides, *Mishneh Torah, The Book of Love*, "Laws of *Tefillin* and *Mezuzah* and the Book of Torah," Chapter 7, Rule no. 1, A commandment upon each and every man of Israel to write down a book of Torah for himself, as it is written, "Now write this song for you" (Deuteronomy 31:19).

32   For more on the topic of *TANTA*, see Baal HaSulam's, "Preface to the Wisdom of Kabbalah," items 46-49, and Rabash, *The Writings of Rabash*, Vol. 3, "TANTA"

33   See Baal HaSulam's essay, "The Essence of the Wisdom of Kabbalah," and *The Study of the Ten Sephirot*, Part 1, "Inner Reflection."

34   For more, see Baal HaSulam's "Introduction to the Study of the Ten Sephirot," Item 22.

35   "If a person enjoys... at that time he is blessing his Maker... And if a person suffers any pain ... though he does not utter condemnation by mouth, the feeling still dominates. This is the title 'Wicked,' for when experiencing any pain, he inevitably condemns ... since the grudge is expressed in the feeling itself and does not need to be revealed in public. And even if he utters a blessing, it is like flattery, similar to the owner beating his slave, and the slave says to him, 'I enjoy the beatings very much, I am overjoyed with all my heart.' It has been said in that regard, 'He who speaks lies shall not be established.'" Baal HaSulam, Letter no. 55

36   "A wicked is one who is still immersed in self-love, for a righteous is called 'good,' and good is called 'bestowal'" (Rabash, *The Writings of Rabash*, Vol. 1, "Who Testifies to a Person").

37   Babylonian Talmud, *Sukkah* 45b

38   "The soul has 613 vessels, called 248 organs and 365 spiritual tendons" Baal HaSulam, "Preface to the Book of Zohar," Item 38

39   "When one can aim in order to bestow, such an act is called a *Mitzva*" (Rabash, *The Writings of Rabash*, Vol. 2, "Concerning

the Reward that We Receive"). For more on the 613 *Mitzvot* according to *The Book of Zohar* (613 counsels and 613 Deposits), see "Introduction to the Book, From the Mouth of a Sage" by Baal HaSulam.

40 Baal HaSulam says about it in *The Writings of the Last Generation* (Part 4, Section 3, "Faith in the Masses"), "They spoiled the meaning of Torah and *Mitzvot*."

41 *Beresheet* Raba, 44:1

42 The matter of repentance is inverting the will to receive to the will to bestow, by which they return to adhesion with their Upper Source, and are rewarded with eternal adhesion ... meaning that the Light of wisdom, perfection, and clarity is revealed" (Rabash, Letter no. 23).

43 In his book, *Yesod Morah* [The Basis of Fear], Eben Ezra refers to the following verses: "The Lord searches every heart" (Chronicles 1, 28:9), "Circumcise the foreskin of your hearts" (Deuteronomy 10:16), and explains that "The Torah was given only to men of heart" (Rabbi Abraham Eben Ezra, *Yesod Morah*, pp 8b-9a).

44 Concerning the difference between the wisdom of Kabbalah and religion, Ramchal said, "The need for the wisdom of truth is indeed great. First, let me tell you that it must be known because we are commanded, for it is written, 'Know this day, and lay it to your heart that the Lord, He is God,' etc.. Thus, we must know, and not only believe, but matters should make sense, as stated explicitly 'and you reformed your heart.' Hence, we should know two things: that the sole Master is the One who governs all, both Above and below; and the other—there is no other, God forbid, meaning to know the truth of His uniqueness. Both these things that we need to know, you tell me, whence will we know them? And which wisdom will teach them to us? We won't be able to understand that from the literal Torah, for on what is the literal Torah founded? Only upon the *Mitzvot*, the manner of carrying them out, and all their ordinances, or upon the narrative of the

- Notes -

actions that took place, which are mentioned there... And if you don't extract that knowing from all those, you must still carry out that *Mitzva*, and you should find a way to keep it. And this is only in this wisdom of truth" (Ramchal, *The Book of Moses' Wars*, "Rules," Rule no. 1).

Rav Chaim Vital, prime disciple and successor of the ARI, emphasized, "The Creator derives no pleasure from all He has created in His world except when His sons below engage in the secrets of Torah to know His greatness, beauty, and merit. It is so because in the literal Torah, in its stories, ordinances, and commandments as they literally are, there is no recognition or knowledge by which to know their Maker, blessed be He. On the contrary, there are commandments and laws in them that the mind cannot tolerate" (*The Writings of the ARI*, "Introduction of Rav Chaim Vital to the Gate of Introductions").

45 Baal HaSulam, *The Writings of the Last Generations*, Part 1, Section 11

46 In the paper *The Nation*, Baal HaSulam describes it as such: "Earth was initially a ball of gases resembling mist. Through the force of gravity in it, it concentrated the atoms in it into a narrower circle for a certain period. In consequence, the ball of gases turned into a liquid ball of fire. Then, over periods of terrible wars between the two forces in Earth, the positive and the negative, the force of coolness overcame the force of the liquid fire, and cooled a thin shell around Earth and encrusted there... Thus, those eras interchanged. Each time the force of coolness prevailed, the shell it overtook became thicker, until the positive forces overcame the negative ones and reached complete harmony: The liquids took their place in the depths of the earth, and the cold shell sufficiently thickened around it, making it possible to create organic life upon it as today."

47 Between the still and the vegetative there is the coral. And between the vegetative and the animate there is *Adnei ha Sadeh* [literally: Bases of the filed]... And between the animate and the speaking is the monkey" (the ARI, *Tree of Life*, Gate 42, Chapter 1. It also appears in Baal HaSulam's *The Study of the Ten Sephirot*, Part 3, Chapter 5, item 3).

48 "It is well known to researchers of Nature that one cannot perform even the slightest movement without motivation, without somehow benefiting oneself. When, for example, one moves one's hand from the chair to the table, it is because one thinks that by putting his hand on the table he will enjoy it more. If he did not think so, he would leave his hand on the chair for the rest of his life without moving it at all. It is all the more so with greater efforts" (Baal HaSulam, "The Peace").

49 Baal HaSulam, *The Study of the Ten Sephirot*, Chapter 1, "Inner Reflection," item 14.

50 "It is written in the Holy *Zohar* that there is a tiny candle that illuminates in the *Klipot* [shells] to sustain them. This means that all the pleasures in the corporeal world are but a sliver of light compared to the delight and pleasure existing in spirituality. Thus, even the lowest degree of spirituality, such as *Nefesh* of *Assiya*, contains more pleasure than all the corporeal pleasures" (Rabash, *The Writings of Rabash*, Vol. 1, "Concerning Happiness"). All the delight and pleasure that the will to receive can receive in its vessels are but a sliver of light compared to the Light that dresses in vessels of bestowal" (Rabash, *The Writings of Rabash*, Vol. 2, "What Is the Significance of the Bridegroom, that His Sins Are Forgiven.") For more on the topic see *The Book of Zohar* with the *Sulam* Commentary, "Introduction of the Book of Zohar," Item 175.)

51 All wars, murder, larceny, and so forth, which exist in the world, are because each one aspires to receive pleasure" (Rabash, *The Writings of Rabash*, Vol. 1, "For Her Sake and Not for Her Sake").

Further Reading

To help you determine which book you would like to read next, we have divided the books into six categories—Beginners, Intermediate, Advanced, Good for All, Textbooks, and For Children. The first three categories are divided by the level of prior knowledge readers are required to have in order to easily relate to the book. The fourth category, Good for All, includes books you can always enjoy, whether you are a complete novice or well versed in Kabbalah.

The fifth category, Textbooks, includes translations of authentic source materials from earlier Kabbalists, such as the Ari, Rav Yehuda Ashlag (Baal HaSulam) and his son and successor, Rav Baruch Ashlag (the Rabash). The category, For Children, includes books that are suitable for children ages three and above. Those are not Kabbalah books per se, but are rather inspired by the teaching and convey the Kabbalistic message of love and unity.

Additional material can be found at www.kabbalah. info. All materials on this site, including e-versions of published books, can be downloaded free of charge.

GOOD FOR ALL

The Secrets of the Eternal Book

The Five Books of Moses (The Torah) are part of the all-time bestselling book, The Bible. Ironically, the Bible is an encoded text. Beneath it lies another level, a hidden subtext that describes the ascent of humanity toward its highest level—the attainment of the Creator.

The Secrets of the Eternal Book decodes some of the Bible's most enigmatic, yet oft-cited epochs, such as the story of Creation, and the Children of Israel's exodus from Egypt.

The author's lively and easygoing style makes for a smooth entrance into the deepest level of reality, where one changes one's world simply by contemplation and desire.

The Kabbalist: a cinematic novel

At the dawn of the deadliest era in human history, the 20th century, a mysterious man appeared carrying a stern warning for humanity and an unlikely solution to its suffering. In his writings, Kabbalist Yehuda Ashlag described in clarity and great detail the wars and upheavals he foresaw, and even more strikingly, the current economic, political, and social crises we are facing today. His deep yearning for a united humanity has driven him to unlock *The Book of Zohar* and make it—and the unique force contained therein—accessible to all.

The Kabbalist is a cinematic novel that will turn on its head everything you thought you knew about Kabbalah, spirituality, freedom of will, and our perception of reality. The book carries a message of unity with scientific clarity and poetic depth. It transcends religion, nationality, mysticism, and the fabric of space and time to show us that the only miracle is the one taking place within, when we begin to act in harmony with Nature and with the entire humanity.

The Point in the Heart:
A Source of Delight for My Soul

The Point in the Heart; a Source of Delight for My Soul is a unique collection of excerpts from a man whose wisdom has earned him devoted students in North America and the world over. Michael Laitman is a scientist, a Kabbalist, and a great thinker who presents ancient wisdom in a compelling style.

This book does not profess to teach Kabbalah, but rather gently introduces ideas from the teaching. *The Point in the Heart* is a window to a new perception. As the author himself testifies to the wisdom of Kabbalah, "It is a science of emotion, a science of pleasure. You are welcome to open and to taste."

Attaining the Worlds Beyond

From the introduction to *Attaining the Worlds Beyond*: "...Not feeling well on the Jewish New Year's Eve of September 1991, my teacher called me to his bedside and handed me his notebook, saying, 'Take it and learn from it.' The following morning, he perished in my arms, leaving me and many of his other disciples without guidance in this world.

"He used to say, 'I want to teach you to turn to the Creator, rather than to me, because He is the only strength, the only Source of all that exists, the only one who can really help you, and He awaits your prayers for help. When you seek help in your search for freedom from the bondage of this world, help in elevating yourself above this world, help in finding the self, and help in determining your purpose in life, you must turn to the Creator, who sends you all those aspirations in order to compel you to turn to Him.'"

Attaining the Worlds Beyond holds within it the content of that notebook, as well as other inspiring texts. This book reaches out to all those seekers who want to find a logical, reliable way to understand the world we live in. This fascinating introduction to the wisdom of Kabbalah will enlighten the mind, invigorate the heart, and move readers to the depths of their souls.

Bail Yourself Out

Bail Yourself Out: how you can emerge strong from the world crisis introduces several extraordinary concepts that weave into a complete solution: 1) The global crisis is essentially not financial, but *psychological*: People have stopped trusting each other, and where there is no trust there is no trade, but only war, isolation, and pain. 2) This mistrust is a result of a *natural process* that's been evolving for millennia and is culminating today. 3) To resolve the crisis, we must first *understand* the process that created the alienation. 4) The first, and most important, step to understanding the crisis is to *inform* people about this natural process through books, such as *Bail Yourself Out*, TV, cinema, and any other means of communication. 5) With this information, we will "*revamp*" our relationships and build them on trust, collaboration, and most importantly, care. This mending process will guarantee that we and our families will prosper in a world of plenty.

Basic Concepts in Kabbalah

This is a book to help readers cultivate an *approach to the concepts* of Kabbalah, to spiritual objects, and to spiritual terms. By reading and re-reading in this book, one develops internal observations, senses, and approaches that did not previously exist within. These newly acquired observations are like sensors that "feel" the space around us that is hidden from our ordinary senses.

Basic Concepts in Kabbalah is intended to foster contemplation of spiritual terms. Once we are integrated with these terms, we can begin to see the unveiling of the spiritual structure that surrounds us, almost as if a mist has been lifted. It is a book for those who wish to awaken the deepest and subtlest sensations they can possess.

Children of Tomorrow: Guidelines for Raising Happy Children in the 21st Century

Children of Tomorrow is a new beginning for you and your children. The big revelation is that raising kids is all about games and play, relating to them as small grownups, and making all major decisions together. You will be surprised to discover how teaching kids about positive things like friendship and caring for others automatically spills into other areas of our lives through the day.

Open any page and you will find thought-provoking quotes about every aspect of children's lives: parent-children relations, friendships and conflicts, and a clear picture of how schools should be designed and function.

The Wise Heart:
Tales and allegories by three contemporary sages

Kabbalah students and enthusiasts in Kabbalah often wonder what the spiritual world actually feels like to a Kabbalist. *The Wise Heart* is a lovingly crafted anthology comprised of tales and allegories by Kabbalist Dr. Michael Laitman, his mentor, Rav Baruch Ashlag (Rabash), and Rabash's father and mentor, Rav Yehuda Ashlag, author of the acclaimed *Sulam* (Ladder) commentary on *The Book of Zohar*. The poems herein offer surprising and often amusing depictions of human nature, with a loving and tender touch that is truly unique to Kabbalists.

FOR CHILDREN

Together Forever: The story about the magician who didn't want to be alone

Like all good children's stories, *Together Forever* transcends boundaries of age, culture, and upbringing. Here, the author tells us that if we are patient and endure the trials we encounter along our life's path, we will become stronger, braver, and wiser.

In this warm, tender tale, Michael Laitman shares with children and parents alike some of the gems and charms of the spiritual world. The wisdom of Kabbalah is filled with spellbinding stories. *Together Forever* is yet another gift from this ageless source of wisdom, whose lessons make our lives richer, easier, and far more fulfilling.

Miracles Can Happen:
Tales for children, but not only...

"Miracles Can Happen," Princes Peony," and "Mary and the Paints" are only three of ten beautiful stories for children ages 3-10. Written especially for children, these short tales convey a single message of love, unity, and care for all beings. The unique illustrations were carefully crafted to contribute to the overall message of the book, and a child who's heard or read any story in this collection is guaranteed to go to sleep smiling.

The Baobab that Opened Its Heart:
and Other Nature Tales for Children

The Baobab that Opened Its Heart is a collection of stories for children, but not just for them. The stories in this collection were written with the love of Nature, of people, and specifically with children in mind. They all share the desire to tell nature's tale of unity, connectedness, and love.

Kabbalah teaches that love is nature's guiding force, the reason for creation. The stories in this book convey it in the unique way that Kabbalah engenders in its students. The variety of authors and diversity of styles allows each reader to find the story that they like most.

BEGINNERS

The Spiritual Roots of the Holy Land

The Spiritual Roots of the Holy Land takes you on a wondrous journey through the land of Israel. As you take in the breathtaking pictures of the holy land, another layer of the age-old country is revealed—its spiritual roots, the ebb and flow of forces that have shaped the curvy landscape that is sacred to billions of people around the world. At the end of the book, you'll find roadmaps of Israel, to help you locate each place you visit, whether in mind or in body, and more details on the forefathers who have made this land the focal point of an entire planet.

Self-Interest vs. Altruism in the Global Era: How society can turn self-interests into mutual benefit

Self-Interest vs. Altruism in the Global Era presents a new perspective on the world's challenges, regarding them as necessary consequences of humanity's growing egotism, rather than a series of errors. In that spirit, the book suggests ways to *use* our egos for society's benefit, rather than trying to suppress them.

...Stating that society's future relies on cooperation of people to work together for society, stating that much of society's degradation in recent decades has been the result of narcissism and greed, *Self Interest vs. Altruism* is a curious and recommended read.

> James A. Cox, Editor-in-Chief,
> Midwest Book Review

A Guide to the Hidden Wisdom of Kabbalah

A Guide to the Hidden Wisdom of Kabbalah is a light and reader-friendly guide to beginners in Kabbalah, covering everything from the history of Kabbalah to how this wisdom can help resolve the world crisis.

The book is set up in three parts: Part 1 covers the history, facts, and fallacies about Kabbalah, and introduces its key concepts. Part 2 tells you all about the spiritual worlds and other neat stuff like the meaning of letters and the power of music. Part 3 covers the implementation of Kabbalah at a time of world crisis.

Kabbalah Revealed: A Guide to a More Peaceful Life

This is the most clearly written, reader-friendly guide to making sense of the surrounding world. Each of its six chapters focuses on a different aspect of the wisdom of Kabbalah, illuminating its teachings and explaining them using various examples from our day-to-day lives.

The first three chapters in *Kabbalah Revealed* explain why the world is in a state of crisis, how our growing desires promote progress as well as alienation, and why the biggest deterrent to achieving positive change is rooted in our own spirits. Chapters Four through Six offer a prescription for positive change. In these chapters, we learn how we can use our spirits to build a personally peaceful life in harmony with all of Creation.

Wondrous Wisdom

This book offers an initial course on Kabbalah. Like all the books presented here, *Wondrous Wisdom* is based solely on authentic teachings passed down from Kabbalist teacher to student over thousands of years. At the heart of the book is a sequence of lessons revealing the nature of Kabbalah's wisdom and explaining how to attain it. For every person questioning "Who am I really?" and "Why am I on this planet?" this book is a must.

Awakening to Kabbalah:
The Guiding Light of Spiritual Fulfillment

A distinctive, personal, and awe-filled introduction to an ancient wisdom tradition. In this book, Rav Laitman offers a deeper understanding of the fundamental teachings of Kabbalah, and how you can use its wisdom to clarify your relationship with others and the world around you.

Using language both scientific and poetic, he probes the most profound questions of spirituality and existence. This provocative, unique guide will inspire and invigorate you to see beyond the world as it is and the limitations of your everyday life, become closer to the Creator, and reach new depths of the soul.

Kabbalah, Science, and the Meaning of Life

Science explains the mechanisms that sustain life; Kabbalah explains why life exists. *Kabbalah, Science, and the Meaning of Life* combines science and spirituality in a captivating dialogue that reveals life's meaning.

For centuries, Kabbalists have been writing that the world is a single entity divided into separate beings. Today the cutting-edge science of quantum physics states a very similar idea: that at the most fundamental level of matter, we are all literally one.

Science proves that reality is affected by the observer who examines it; and so does Kabbalah. But Kabbalah makes an even bolder statement: even the Creator, the Maker of reality, is within the observer.

These earthshaking concepts and more are eloquently introduced so that even readers new to Kabbalah or science will easily understand them. So if you are curious about why you are here, what life means, and what you can do to enjoy it more, this book is for you.

From Chaos to Harmony

Many researchers and scientists agree that the ego is the reason behind the perilous state our world is in today. Laitman's groundbreaking book not only demonstrates that egoism has been the basis for all suffering throughout human history, but also shows how we can turn our plight to pleasure.

The book contains a clear analysis of the human soul and its problems, and provides a "roadmap" of what we need to do to once again be happy. *From*

Chaos to Harmony explains how we can rise to a new level of existence on personal, social, national, and international levels.

Kabbalah for Beginners

Kabbalah for Beginners is a book for all those seeking answers to life's essential questions. We all want to know why we are here, why there is pain, and how we can make life more enjoyable. The four parts of this book provide us with reliable answers to these questions, as well as clear explanations of the gist of Kabbalah and its practical implementations.

Part One discusses the discovery of the wisdom of Kabbalah, and how it was developed, and finally concealed until our time. Part Two introduces the gist of the wisdom of Kabbalah, using ten easy drawings to help us understand the structure of the spiritual worlds, and how they relate to our world. Part Three reveals Kabbalistic concepts that are largely unknown to the public, and Part Four elaborates on practical means you and I can take, to make our lives better and more enjoyable for us and for our children.

INTERMEDIATE

The Kabbalah Experience

The depth of the wisdom revealed in the questions and answers within this book will inspire readers to reflect and contemplate. This is not a book to race through, but rather one that should be read thoughtfully and carefully. With this approach, readers will begin to experience a growing sense of enlightenment while simply absorbing the answers to the questions every Kabbalah student asks along the way.

The Kabbalah Experience is a guide from the past to the future, revealing situations that all students of Kabbalah will experience at some point along their journeys. For those who cherish every moment in life, this book offers unparalleled insights into the timeless wisdom of Kabbalah.

The Path of Kabbalah

This unique book combines beginners' material with more advanced concepts and teachings. If you have read a book or two of Laitman's, you will find this book very easy to relate to.

While touching upon basic concepts such as perception of reality and Freedom of Choice, *The Path of Kabbalah* goes deeper and expands beyond the scope of beginners' books. The structure of the worlds, for example, is explained in greater detail here than in the "pure" beginners' books. Also described is the spiritual root of mundane matters such as the Hebrew calendar and the holidays.

ADVANCED

The Science of Kabbalah

Kabbalist and scientist Rav Michael Laitman, PhD, designed this book to introduce readers to the special language and terminology of the authentic wisdom of Kabbalah. Here, Rav Laitman reveals authentic Kabbalah in a manner both rational and mature. Readers are gradually led to understand the logical design of the Universe and the life that exists in it.

The Science of Kabbalah, a revolutionary work unmatched in its clarity, depth, and appeal to the intellect, will enable readers to approach the more technical works of Baal HaSulam (Rabbi Yehuda Ashlag), such as *The Study of the Ten Sefirot* and *The Book of Zohar*. Readers of this book will enjoy the satisfying answers to the riddles of life that only authentic Kabbalah provides. Travel through the pages and prepare for an astonishing journey into the Upper Worlds.

Introduction to the Book of Zohar

This volume, along with *The Science of Kabbalah*, is a required preparation for those who wish to understand the hidden message of *The Book of Zohar*. Among the many helpful topics dealt with in this text is an introduction to the "language of roots and branches," without which the stories in *The Zohar* are mere fable and legend. *Introduction to the Book of Zohar* will provide readers with the necessary tools to understand authentic Kabbalah as it was originally meant to be—as a means to attain the Upper Worlds.

The Book of Zohar: annotations to the Ashlag commentary

The Book of Zohar is an age-old source of wisdom and the basis for all Kabbalistic literature. Since its appearance, it has been the primary, and often only source used by Kabbalists.

Written in a unique and metaphorical language, *The Book of Zohar* enriches our understanding of reality and widens our worldview. Rav Yehuda Ashlag's unique

Sulam (Ladder) commentary allows us to grasp the hidden meanings of the text and "climb" toward the lucid perceptions and insights that the book holds for those who study it.

TEXTBOOKS

Shamati (I Heard)

Rav Michael Laitman's words on the book: "Among all the texts and notes that were used by my teacher, Rav Baruch Shalom Halevi Ashlag (the Rabash), there was one special notebook he always carried. This notebook contained transcripts of his conversations with his father, Rav Yehuda Leib Halevi Ashlag (Baal HaSulam), author of the *Sulam* (Ladder) commentary on *The Book of Zohar*, *The Study of the Ten Sefirot* (a commentary on the texts of the Kabbalist, Ari), and many other works on Kabbalah.

"Not feeling well on the Jewish New Year's Eve of September 1991, the Rabash summoned me to his bedside and handed me a notebook, whose cover contained only one word, *Shamati* (I Heard). As he handed the notebook, he said, 'Take it and learn from it.' The following morning, my teacher perished in my arms, leaving me and many of his other disciples without guidance in this world.

Committed to Rabash's legacy to disseminate the wisdom of Kabbalah, I published the notebook just as it was written, thus retaining the text's transforming powers. Among all the books of Kabbalah, *Shamati* is a unique and compelling creation."

Kabbalah for the Student

Kabbalah for the Student offers authentic texts by Rav Yehuda Ashlag, author of the *Sulam* (Ladder) commentary on *The Book of Zohar*, his son and successor, Rav Baruch Ashlag, as well as other great Kabbalists. It also offers illustrations that accurately depict the evolution of the Upper Worlds as Kabbalists experience them. The book also contains several explanatory essays that help us understand the texts within.

In *Kabbalah for the Student*, Rav Michael Laitman, PhD, Rav Baruch Ashlag's personal assistant and prime student, compiled all the texts a Kabbalah student would need in order to attain the spiritual worlds. In his daily lessons, Rav Laitman bases his teaching on these inspiring texts, thus helping novices and veterans alike to better understand the spiritual path we undertake on our fascinating journey to the Higher Realms.

Rabash—the Social Writings

Rav Baruch Shalom HaLevi Ashlag (Rabash) played a remarkable role in the history of Kabbalah. He provided us with the necessary final link connecting the wisdom of Kabbalah to our human experience. His father and teacher was the great Kabbalist, Rav Yehuda Leib HaLevi Ashlag, known as Baal HaSulam for his *Sulam* (Ladder) commentary on *The Book of Zohar*. Yet, if not for the essays of Rabash, his father's efforts to disclose the wisdom of Kabbalah to all would have been in vain. Without those essays, few would be able to achieve the spiritual attainment that Baal HaSulam so desperately wanted us to obtain.

The writings in this book aren't just for reading. They are more like an experiential user's guide. It is very important to work with them in order to see what they truly contain. The reader should try to put them into practice by living out the emotions Rabash so masterfully describes. He always advised his students to summarize the articles, to work with the texts, and those who attempt it discover that it always yields new insights. Thus, readers are advised to work with the texts, summarize them, translate them, and implement them in the group. Those who do so will discover the power in the writings of Rabash.

Gems of Wisdom:
Words of the great Kabbalists from all generations

Through the millennia, Kabbalists have bequeathed us with numerous writings. In their compositions, they have laid out a structured method that can lead, step by step, unto a world of eternity and wholeness.

Gems of wisdom is a collection of selected excerpts from the writings of the greatest Kabbalists from all generations, with particular emphasis on the writings of Rav Yehuda Leib HaLevi Ashlag (Baal HaSulam), author of the *Sulam* [Ladder] commentary of *The Book of Zohar*.

The sections have been arranged by topics, to provide the broadest view possible on each topic. This book is a useful guide to any person desiring spiritual advancement.

Let There Be Light:
Selected excerpts from The Book of Zohar

The Zohar contains all the secrets of Creation, but until recently the wisdom of Kabbalah was locked under a thousand locks. Thanks to the work of Rav Yehuda Ashlag (1884-1954), the last of the great Kabbalists, *The Zohar* is revealed today in order to propel humanity to its next degree.

Let There Be Light contains selected excerpts from the series *Zohar for All*, a refined edition of *The Book of Zohar* with the *Sulam* commentary. Each piece was carefully chosen for its beauty and depth as well as its capacity to draw the reader into *The Zohar* and get the most out of the reading experience. As *The Zohar* speaks of nothing but the intricate web that connects all souls, diving into its words attracts the special force that exists in that state of oneness, where we are all connected.

About Bnei Baruch

B nei Baruch is an international group of Kabbalists who share the wisdom of Kabbalah with the entire world. The study materials (in over 30 languages) are authentic Kabbalah texts that were passed down from generation to generation.

HISTORY AND ORIGIN

In 1991, following the passing of his teacher, Rav Baruch Shalom HaLevi Ashlag (The Rabash), Michael Laitman, Professor of Ontology and the Theory of Knowledge, PhD in Philosophy and Kabbalah, and MSc in Medical Bio-Cybernetics, established a Kabbalah study group called "Bnei Baruch." He called it Bnei Baruch (Sons of Baruch) to commemorate his mentor, whose side he never left in the final twelve years of his life, from 1979 to 1991. Dr. Laitman had been Ashlag's prime student and personal assistant, and is recognized as the successor to Rabash's teaching method.

The Rabash was the firstborn son and successor of Rav Yehuda Leib HaLevi Ashlag, the greatest Kabbalist of the 20th century. Rav Ashlag authored the most authoritative and comprehensive commentary on *The Book of Zohar*, titled *The Sulam* (Ladder) *Commentary*. He was the first to reveal the complete method for spiritual ascent, and thus was known as Baal HaSulam (Owner of the Ladder).

Bnei Baruch bases its entire study method on the path paved by these two great spiritual leaders.

THE STUDY METHOD

The unique study method developed by Baal HaSulam and his son, the Rabash, is taught and applied on a daily basis by Bnei Baruch. This method relies on authentic Kabbalah sources such as *The Book of Zohar*, by Rabbi Shimon Bar-Yochai, *The Tree of Life*, by the Ari, and *The Study of the Ten Sefirot*, by Baal HaSulam.

While the study relies on authentic Kabbalah sources, it is carried out in simple language and uses a scientific, contemporary approach. The unique combination of an academic study method and personal experiences broadens the students' perspective and awards them a new perception of the reality they live in. Those on the spiritual path are thus given the necessary tools to study themselves and their surrounding reality.

Bnei Baruch is a diverse movement of tens of thousands of students worldwide. Students can choose their own paths and intensity of their studies according to their unique conditions and abilities.

THE MESSAGE

The essence of the message disseminated by Bnei Baruch is universal: unity of the people, unity of nations and love of man.

For millennia, Kabbalists have been teaching that love of man should be the foundation of all human relations. This love prevailed in the days of Abraham, Moses, and the group of Kabbalists that they established. If we make room for these seasoned, yet contemporary values, we will discover that we possess the power to put differences aside and unite.

The wisdom of Kabbalah, hidden for millennia, has been waiting for the time when we would be sufficiently developed and ready to implement its message. Now, it is emerging as a solution that can unite diverse factions everywhere, enabling us, as individuals and as a society, to meet today's challenges.

ACTIVITIES

Bnei Baruch was established on the premise that "only by expansion of the wisdom of Kabbalah to the public can we be awarded complete redemption" (Baal HaSulam). Therefore, Bnei Baruch offers a variety of ways for people to explore and discover the purpose of their lives, providing careful guidance for beginners and advanced students alike.

Internet

Bnei Baruch's international website, www.kab.info, presents the authentic wisdom of Kabbalah using essays, books, and original texts. It is by far the most expansive source of authentic Kabbalah material on the Internet, containing a unique, extensive library for readers to thoroughly explore the wisdom of Kabbalah. Additionally, the media archive, www.kabbalahmedia. info, contains thousands of media items, downloadable books, and a vast reservoir of texts, video and audio files in many languages.

Bnei Baruch's online Kabbalah Education Center offers free Kabbalah courses for beginners, initiating students into this profound body of knowledge in the comfort of their own homes.

Dr. Laitman's daily lessons are also aired live on www.kab.tv, along with complementary texts and diagrams.

All these services are provided free of charge.

Television

In Israel, Bnei Baruch established its own channel, no. 66 on both cable and satellite, which broadcasts 24/7 Kabbalah TV. The channel is also aired on the Internet at www.kab.tv. All broadcasts on the channel are free of charge. Programs are adapted for all levels, from complete beginners to the most advanced.

Conferences

Twice a year, students gather for a weekend of study and socializing at conferences in various locations in the U.S., as well as an annual convention in Israel. These gatherings provide a great setting for meeting like-minded people, for bonding, and for expanding one's understanding of the wisdom.

Kabbalah Books

Bnei Baruch publishes authentic books, written by Baal HaSulam, his son, the Rabash, as well as books by Dr. Michael Laitman. The books of Rav Ashlag and Rabash are essential for complete understanding of the teachings of authentic Kabbalah, explained in Laitman's lessons.

Dr. Laitman writes his books in a clear, contemporary style based on the key concepts of Baal HaSulam. These books are a vital link between today's readers and the original texts. All the books are available for sale, as well as for free download.

Paper

Kabbalah Today is a free paper produced and disseminated by Bnei Baruch in many languages, including English, Hebrew, Spanish, and Russian. It is apolitical, non-commercial, and written in a clear, contemporary style. The purpose of *Kabbalah Today* is to expose the vast knowledge hidden in the wisdom of Kabbalah at no cost and in a clear, engaging style for readers everywhere.

Kabbalah Lessons

As Kabbalists have been doing for centuries, Laitman gives a daily lesson. The lessons are given in Hebrew and are simultaneously interpreted into seven languages—English, Russian, Spanish, French, German, Italian, and Turkish—by skilled and experienced interpreters. As with everything else, the live broadcast is free of charge.

FUNDING

Bnei Baruch is a non-profit organization for teaching and sharing the wisdom of Kabbalah. To maintain its independence and purity of intentions, Bnei Baruch is not supported, funded, or otherwise tied to any government or political organization.

Since the bulk of its activity is provided free of charge, the prime sources of funding for the group's activities are donations and tithing—contributed by students on a voluntary basis—and Dr. Laitman's books, which are sold at cost.

CONTACT INFORMATION

1057 Steeles Avenue West, Suite 532
Toronto, ON, M2R 3X1
Canada

Bnei Baruch USA,
2009 85th street, #51,
Brooklyn, New York, 11214
USA

E-mail: info@kabbalah.info
Web site: www.kabbalah.info

Toll free in USA and Canada:
1-866-LAITMAN
Fax: 1-905 886 9697